SINCE

SINCE THE COMING OF STALIN,

THE WORLD HAS BEEN CONCERNED WITH COMMUNISM AND THE RUSSIAN PEOPLE

In 1919 Winston Churchill said, "RUSSIA, LIKE ALL GREAT NATIONS, IS INDESTRUCTIBLE. EITHER SHE MUST CONTINUE TO SUFFER AND HER SUFFERINGS WILL DISTURB AND CONVULSE THE WHOLE WORLD, OR SHE MUST BE RESCUED . . . I SAY TO THE THOUGHTLESS, I SAY TO THE UNINSTRUCTED, I SAY TO THE SIMPLE, I SAY TO THE BUSY—YOU MAY ABANDON RUSSIA, BUT RUSSIA WILL NOT ABANDON YOU . . . YOU CANNOT REMAKE THE WORLD WITHOUT RUSSIA. YOU CANNOT GO ON INTO VICTORY AND PROSPERITY AND PEACE AND LEAVE THAT VAST PROPORTION OF THE HUMAN RACE SUFFERING TORTURE IN THE NIGHT OF BARBARISM."

STALIN

A PHOTO HISTORY OF OUR TIME

by Boris Shub and Bernard Quint

SWEN PUBLICATIONS CO. INC.
NEW YORK • MANILA • *1951*

*Engraved, Printed and Bound by Union Labor in the United States of America
Type Composition and Letterpress Printing by The Condé Nast Press.
Photoengravings by Wilbar Photo Engraving Company, Inc.
Bound by H. Wolff Book Manufacturing Company, Inc.
Format and Layouts by Bernard Quint*

ACKNOWLEDGMENT

A book dealing with such varied aspects of history as does SINCE STALIN inevitably requires the assistance of many individuals and institutions. First among our acknowledgments is:

To the many photographers who have helped preserve the record of the people and events with which this book is concerned;

To the editors of LIFE, whose generosity has been invaluable;

To Anatole Shub, for his decisive editing of the manuscript;

To Natalie Kosek, for thorough and untiring picture research;

To Margaret Hamilton Redman, Beverly Baff and Elizabeth Charney, for their understanding and their loyal assistance.

Preparing this book, we discovered that many of the documents required to tell the story of SINCE STALIN had been deliberately destroyed, suppressed, or (in the case of public libraries) mysteriously removed. We must thank many anonymous individuals for documents or clues which helped us overcome this obstacle. In this connection, we would like to express our gratitude to Vladimir Gsovski of the Library of Congress.

Finally, we wish to express our gratitude to the publisher for his rare patience and cooperation.

WAR OR PEACE

The Russian at left, the people

Two world wars this century have taken 30,000,000 lives without solving any basic problems. Neither the American people nor the Russian people, in the shadow of whose might stand the nations of the world, wants a third war. "The peoples of both our countries," President Truman told Russia on July 8, 1951, "know from personal experience the horror and misery of war.

They abhor the thought of a future conflict which they know would be waged by means of the most hideous weapons in the history of mankind." Survival, most men realize, requires cooperation among peoples; it requires that governments adhere to the elementary code which civilized men honor in their daily lives. After World War I, men looked to the League of Nations to

of the world, and the American at right all are against war but only a free people can choose

enforce such a code. Since 1945, they have expected the United Nations to do so. Yet now, as always, some rulers have lived by a code of their own and have prevented their people from living in peace with others. A people free to choose between war and peace will always choose peace; but rulers who defy their people's will cannot live in peace with anyone. In our time, rulers who live at war with their own subjects menace the entire world. One such despot, Adolf Hitler, plunged mankind into six years of war. Hitler is dead, but others such still exist. If a third world war is to be averted, all must know who is obstructing the universal will to peace, so that all may act together for their common safety. They must know **WHO IS RESPONSIBLE?**

OUR TIME BEGINS IN 1903, WITH THE BIRTH OF THIS MAN'S PARTY

THIS MAN and his men have
serious business in every corner of the world

The marchers on the left are Chinese. They could be Germans, Russians, Americans or Indonesians. The smiling man above has followers in every corner of the world. His party's world-wide affiliates, united in an international bureau, are subordinate to his will; its functionaries, whether Czech security officers or French scientists, accept his authority. In large areas of the world, they hold absolute power over hundreds of millions of people. Other rulers, though sworn to fight his party, have accepted its doctrine that men and women exist for the state and have no inviolable rights of their own. Even in countries where freedom stands, the force of this doctrine has corroded belief in freedom. Many fear that history is on his side and that all peoples must inevitably meet his system halfway. On the other hand, many more reject his party's code and await the world triumph of liberty. They believe that this man and his party represent an obstacle to peace—a tyranny that threatens mankind with another war. What are the facts? **HOW DID IT BEGIN?**

GEORGIA, Stalin's native country, lies on the Black Sea in the snow-peaked mountains of the Caucasus which divide Europe and Asia.

THE BOY grew up in Georgia, studied theology, rebelled against old Russia

Joseph Vissarionovitch "Stalin," whose real name is Djugashvili, was born in Gori, Georgia, on December 21, 1879. Twenty-five centuries ago, Georgia had a higher civilization than most of Europe; Christianized before England or France, it reached its cultural peak around 1150. Plunderings by Mongols, Persians and Turks forced it to seek protection from Christian Russia; in 1801 it became part of the empire. Under Tsarist rule, the proud Georgians struggled to keep their culture. Stalin spoke Georgian at home; he learned Russian in school, but he still retains his native accent. He left Gori in 1894 to study at the Greek Theological Seminary in Tiflis, Georgia's capital, and remained there five years. Discipline was harsh; reading forbidden books was punished by confinement in a cell. An ex-student complained that they were "locked in day and night, within barracks walls ... like prisoners who must spend years there, without being guilty of anything." Stalin rebelled against what he later called "the rigorous intolerance and jesuitical discipline" of the seminary. He attended radical meetings in the city, and secretly read Hugo, Darwin and Karl Marx. In 1899, he left the seminary to become a professional revolutionary.

GEORGIANS, of Iberian stock with later Oriental strains, became Orthodox Christians in the 4th century; they retain their language.

GORI, where Stalin was born and attended church school until he was 14, saw fierce blood-feuds among Georgians, Tartars and Armenians.

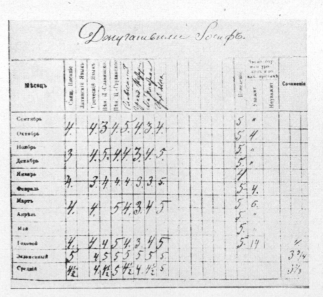

STALIN'S report card shows that he was best (5 is top mark) in liturgy and conduct, good in Scriptures and Church Slavonic, fair in Russian composition; it also shows 14 absences in his first year at the seminary.

HUT where Stalin was born had one dimly lit room and a kitchen. A straw mattress covered the over-sized plank bed. The floor was brick. On rainy days, mud and water seeped in from the drab courtyard. Today it is a marble-encased museum surrounded by flower beds.

CATHEDRAL of Vasili the Blessed, built in the 16th century to celebrate Russia's liberation from the Tartars, overlooks Red Square.

ORTHODOX CHURCH and its stately processions influenced Russia for nearly 1000 years. Religion was an important part of daily life.

OLD SYMBOLS

still stood, but new industry, peasant education

At the turn of the century, when Stalin began his career, visitors to Russia were still fascinated by the contrast between the splendor of the church and court and the poverty of the peasants. Few realized that the industrial revolution was already transforming the land. Large textile, metallurgical and mining industries were being developed; oil fields were springing up in the Caucasus. Count Witte, the Finance Minister from 1892 to 1903, drove the Trans-Siberian railroad from the modern capital of St. Petersburg (later Petrograd, now Leningrad) to the Pacific port of Vladivostok. Social reforms were also fermenting. Serfdom had been abolished in 1861. Three years later, self-governing rural councils, known as Zemstvos, first offered

OF POWER

and railroads were transforming Russian life

the peasants secular education, hospital care and other civic benefits. The same year also introduced independent courts and trial by public jury. The 80's brought laws for the protection of child and female labor; the 90's saw limits set on hours of factory work. Such changes weakened the caste barriers which had buttressed the Romanovs for nearly 300 years and stirred popular demands for constitutional government. But Nicholas II, who had become Tsar in 1894, dismissed them as "idle dreams" and clung to his autocratic power, supported by the Holy Synod and the gentry. Whenever he wavered, his superstitious wife, the Empress Alexandra (née Alix of Hesse-Darmstadt), reminded him that he was "Autocrat of All the Russias."

BOMBS expressed the most extreme protest against autocracy. One such bomb killed Alexander II in 1881; this explosion killed a horse.

COUNT Muraviev-Apostol, a leader of December 1825 revolt, had been stirred by the revolutions in France and America.

PUSHKIN, one of world's greatest poets, immortalized the Decembrists and wrote, "In my ruthless age, I glorified freedom."

MOUSSORGSKY gave opera new dramatic realism. His music carried Pushkin's *Boris Godunov* far outside of Russia.

THE TITANS who stirred

Russia gave new dimensions to man's thought

In the century from the end of the Napoleonic wars to the democratic March Revolution of 1917, Russia produced titans of science, literature, music, the theater and the ballet, while her philosophers waged moral war against political, social and economic injustice. The first great poet, Alexander Pushkin, was close to the Decembrists, a group of officers who revolted against autocracy in 1825. Nicholas Gogol's grim satire, *Dead Souls*, contributed to the abolition of serfdom. His *Inspector General* exposed bureaucratic corruption to merciless ridicule. Of Ivan Turgenev, the French philosopher Renan said, "Generations of ancestors, lost, speechless, in the sleep of centuries, have come to life and found utterance through him." Leo Tolstoy and Fyodor Dostoevsky combined profound realism with moral passion. Such books as *War and Peace, Anna Karenina, Crime and Punishment* and *The Brothers Karamazov* dominated the intellectual life of several decades and continue to influence literature throughout the western world. A humanitarian spirit was the main force that surged through Russia's cultural awakening.

METCHNIKOFF (left), with Tolstoy in 1907. His discovery of white phagocytes in blood expanded the knowledge of disease. Among Russian scientists, he ranks with Lobachevsky, founder of non-Euclidean geometry, and Mendeleyev, author of the *Periodic Law of Elements*.

HERZEN, a radical writer, warned in 1867 that socialism without liberty "would soon degenerate into autocratic communism."

CHEKHOV, master of the short story and drama, collaborated with Stanislavsky to develop Moscow's famous Art Theater.

DOSTOEVSKY went deep into the mind to discover man's capacity for self-destruction and his interminable search for justice.

LENIN, born in Simbirsk on the Volga in 1870, is shown here at nine (front right, with family). His older brother (back center) was hanged in 1887 for an attempt to kill the Tsar. Their mother was of German descent; she reared all her children, one of them wrote, "to a certain extent in the German tradition."

THE HOUSE WHERE LENIN WAS BORN

THE PARTY Stalin joined

split when Lenin demanded centralized control

The desire for freedom was the spark that ignited the Russian revolutionary movement and kept it burning through the 19th and early 20th centuries. The first rebel democrat, Alexander Radishchev (1749-1802), made George Washington the hero of his *Ode to Freedom* and was exiled to Siberia by Empress Catherine II because "he hails Benjamin Franklin." The Decembrists (1825), who followed Radishchev, modeled their projected federal constitution along American lines and proclaimed, "The division into nobles and common people is herewith rejected, in so far as it is against Faith, according to which all men are brothers, all are born noble at God's will, all are born for happiness." Original Russian socialist ideas which emphasized peasant action and had the largest popular support found political outlet in the People's Will Party (founded 1879) and in its successor, the Socialist Revolutionaries (1902). They demanded that the Tsar surrender his autocratic power to a Constituent Assembly elected by free and universal suffrage. They rejected the Marxist doctrine of a "proletarian dictatorship." The founders of Marxism in Russia, George Plekhanov, Vera Zasulich, and Paul Axelrod, regarded the new industrial working class as the main instrument of political and social progress, but they also came to oppose one-party dictatorship. In 1898 the Russian Marxists organized the Social Democratic Labor Party. Two years later the party began to publish, in Germany, a clandestine newspaper, *Iskra* (Spark), for distribution in Russia. One of its editors was Lenin. The secret network of agents which distributed copies of *Iskra* among students and factory workers became the nucleus of the Marxist underground. At their second Congress, held in London in 1903, the Social Democrats split into two factions, Bolsheviks (majority) and Mensheviks (minority). Lenin, the Bolshevik leader, demanded that membership be restricted to those who would accept a rigid party discipline, while the Mensheviks favored admitting everyone who supported the party's general program. All the future battles between Communists and democratic socialists were foreshadowed in this break. The Mensheviks often sided with the liberal Constitutional Democratic Party (founded in 1903) and concentrated on the achievement of political freedom and practical social reforms. Lenin, for his part, insisted that the "dictatorship of the proletariat" would give the people greater political freedom than they enjoyed under "bourgeois democracy." This ambiguous claim enabled Lenin to rally support among workers who believed he stood for more freedom than his democratic adversaries. Lenin himself may well have believed so at the start, but as he struggled for power, he became more and more authoritarian, less and less tolerant of the slightest deviation from Marxist doctrine, which he called "the objective truth." In distant Georgia, Stalin sided almost from the first with Lenin.

POLICE RECORD on Lenin began with his first arrest in 1895. Lenin was to spend the next five years in prison and Siberia. But the police didn't take the Marxists seriously. "A small clique," one official said in a report; "nothing will come of them for at least fifty years."

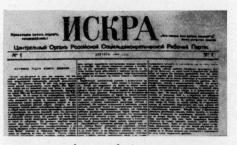

ISKRA was the revolutionary newspaper started by Lenin and other Marxists in Germany on December 21, 1900. Printed on flimsy paper, it was smuggled into Russia.

GEORGE PLEKHANOV, pioneer of Marxism in Russia, backed Lenin in 1903, but soon clashed with him over *Iskra's* editorial policy. In 1904, Lenin started his own paper.

VERA FIGNER helped kill Tsar Alexander II, but seven months later, she condemned the murder of President Garfield, stating that violence was unjustified in a democracy.

GEORGIAN socialists were led by Stalin's first teacher, Noah Jordania. He opposed Lenin at the 1903 Congress. Most Georgian workers thenceforth supported the Mensheviks.

CONFLICT between the human being and the political fanatic is clearly revealed in these notes which Lenin made at the London Congress. He warns against admitting liberals like Peter Struve into the party. In heavy characters, he demands "narrowing the circle" and calls for a party of professional revolutionaries. An angry arrow brands the arguments of the moderates as "harmful." But, homesick for the Russian countryside after more than three years abroad, he prints the word *berioza* (birch tree) three times in neat letters.

SIEGE GUNS of Japanese pound Port Arthur. The Russian garrison held out almost a year.

SURPRISE defeat by Japan hits prestige of Tsar Nicholas at home and abroad

Tsar Nicholas II's reactionary advisers believed that a quick, victorious war would divert public attention and lessen the popular pressure for reforms. Tsarist political intrigues in Korea provoked Japan to strike, on February 8, 1904, without declaring war. Most Russians greeted with indifference or even hostility this conflict over foreign territory in the distant Orient. Japan had bases close to home, while the Russian army had to travel thousands of miles over the Trans-Siberian railway to reach the battlefront. Decisive Japanese victories on land (Port Arthur) and sea (Tsushima) made Nicholas willing to accept an American offer of mediation. Japan emerged as a world power, while the Tsar's position at home and abroad was undermined by the heavy losses inflicted on the Russian army and navy.

PEACEMAKER of the Russo-Japanese conflict, President Theodore Roosevelt persuaded both parties to conclude a treaty at Portsmouth, New Hampshire, on September 5, 1905. Foreign Minister Witte (left) signed for Russia, Marquis Komura (in doorway) for Japan.

CAPTURED by the thousands in the distant hills of Manchuria and Korea (as above), the Tsar's apathetic soldiers failed to score the

expected easy victory over the "backward Asiatics." A succession of military disasters, precipitated by corrupt, incompetent leadership, demonstrated to the whole world the weakness of the Tsarist regime and stoked the flames of political discontent in Russia.

PETITION for reforms was brought to the Tsar's Winter Palace by the populace led by Father Gapon (center). "Despotism and arbitrary rule throttle us," they protested.

MASSACRE of the peaceful crowd by imperial troops on famous Bloody Sunday outraged

STALIN LED STRIKES IN GEORGIA

Revolution in **1905** forces fearful Tsar to grant

In November 1904, the All-Russian Zemstvo Congress demanded civil liberty and a representative assembly. These demands, echoing in St. Petersburg, brought on the infamous "Bloody Sunday" massacre of January 22, 1905.

Finally, a nationwide strike forced the Tsar to issue a manifesto on October 30, 1905, granting civil liberties and elections to an Imperial Duma (parliament). Meanwhile a Soviet (council) of Workers' Deputies in St. Petersburg demanded

BANNERS of Bolsheviks in Moscow cried "Down with autocracy—we demand a Constituent Assembly," at funeral of Bauman, a worker killed in the December struggle.

UPRISING in Moscow, approved by Lenin, came a few weeks after Tsar had granted a

all Russia. Henceforth, millions knew the weak-willed Tsar as "Nicholas the Bloody."

MUTINY on the cruiser *Potemkin* (June 14, 1905) led to other revolts at Kronstadt and

Sevastopol naval bases. The revolutionary wave spread to workers in key industries.

a constitution, but continued turmoil paves way for strong man

a republican Constituent Assembly— young Leon Trotsky, then a Menshevik, was one of its leaders. When Moscow workers fought on the barricades that December, Plekhanov condemned them, but Lenin replied, "Those who do not prepare for armed uprising must be ruthlessly cast out of the ranks of the supporters of the revolution." New outbreaks, and a Bolshevik campaign against the Duma, emboldened the Tsar to name a strong man, Peter Stolypin, his Premier.

TROTSKY LED SOVIET IN CAPITAL

Constitution. Such violence alarmed moderates and split Russia's democratic forces.

DUMA, dissolved by the Tsar when its majority proved liberal, met secretly in Viborg

woods and urged the people to keep fighting for a truly representative government.

PRIESTS joined the fight for freedom. Father Petrov (left) was a Constitutional Democratic deputy to the Second Duma; Father Kolokolnikov (right), a Socialist Revolutionary deputy. Workers and peasants read more than ten million copies of Petrov's moral and political pamphlets. He wrote: "While the common people want light as grass wants the sun, the nobility are a separate race entirely; they cannot understand the wants of the people." Although he preached to Imperial Grand Dukes, Petrov was unfrocked by the Holy Synod.

PEASANTS chose their own vigorous spokesmen (peasant deputies of the Second Duma above). The Peasants' Union had played an important part in the Revolution of 1905. The Socialist Revolutionary Party, which was active in the villages, had strong peasant following.

SUNDAY STROLLERS through Catherine Square in St. Petersburg (1910) enjoy the mild weather while the new dirigible *Dove* flies overhead.

REFORMS of new parliament
improve life while Russians seek more freedom

When the First Duma met on May 10, 1906, the liberal Constitutional Democratic majority presented a broad reform program which included social security legislation, equality for national and religious minorities, and the expropriation of crown lands and large estates for distribution among the peasants. Plekhanov urged workers to support the Duma, but Lenin told them to "unmask the liberal counter-revolutionary Constitutional Democrats" and prepare for insurrection. The Tsar dissolved the Duma in July and ordered new elections, but the Second Duma had an even stronger anti-government majority—the Social Democrats and Socialist Revolutionaries held 120 of the 524 seats. When Lenin demanded that the Social Democratic deputies use their parliamentary immunity to organize an armed uprising, Prime Minister Stolypin produced a document, forged by the secret police (Okhrana), linking the Social Democrats with Lenin's program. He ordered the arrest for treason of the Social Democratic deputies—a group of them, headed by Iracli Tseretelli, were condemned to hard labor in Siberia—and again dissolved parliament, in June 1907. Stolypin now felt strong enough to revise the election law to favor the propertied classes, so the Third Duma (1907-1912) had a safe Conservative majority. But although Stolypin was ruthless with the Socialists, he was shrewd enough to accept a number of important social reforms initiated by the Duma. The Third Duma's universal education program increased the number of grade schools from 100,000 in 1908 to 150,000 in 1913; the 1914 educational budget was seven times higher than it had been twenty years earlier; within another decade, there would be classrooms for every child in Russia. A 1905 law gave the universities almost complete academic freedom; their attendance rose steadily, and their academic standards were on a par with Europe's best. Labor laws limited work on railroads to nine hours a day and sharply curtailed night work in industry. A health and accident insurance law passed in 1912. Foreign capital had predominated in Russia at the turn of the century, but commerce and industry were largely in native hands by 1910. Living standards rose with general economic progress; between 1900 and 1913, there was a 15 per cent increase in the purchasing power of the wage earner.

BOLSHEVIK KAMO (right) staged Tiflis bank holdup in June 1907 under the direction of the Party's Caucasian Bureau. It netted 341,000 roubles for Party use, but Bolsheviks like Maxim Litvinov who tried to pass the bills abroad were arrested. Stalin (1910 police photo) was Lenin's liaison between the Bureau and the bands which executed such crimes. Although Social Democratic leaders abroad and in Georgia attacked Lenin and Stalin for using these methods, Lenin was very much impressed by his Georgian aide's resourcefulness.

LAND REFORM was Premier Stolypin's project for reducing revolutionary discontent, by trying to create a strong class of independent farmers. In 1907 his agrarian legislation had called for the gradual disappearance of the old system of communal peasant holdings; under the new laws, every member of the commune was given the right to convert his strips in the common land of the village into a single consolidated farm. By the end of 1913, almost a fourth of all peasant households in European Russia had

FOURTH DUMA (1912-1917) emphasized the trend against the old regime. Government deputies veered toward the Constitutional Democrats. Laborite Alexander Kerensky won a national reputation as the spokesman of anti-Tsarist sentiment. The July 1914 political strikes in St. Petersburg also reflected the people's desire for full freedom.

RECLAMATION projects improved conditions of the peasants. Liberal homestead laws encouraged them to settle reclaimed land. By 1914, they held three-fourths of the arable

become independent farms. The popular demand for expropriating the large estates continued, nevertheless. The photo shows peasants drawing their land shares by lot.

acreage, but some of the best was still owned by large export combines. Above, the sluice of a new irrigation project in the "hungry steppe" of Central Asia, 1913.

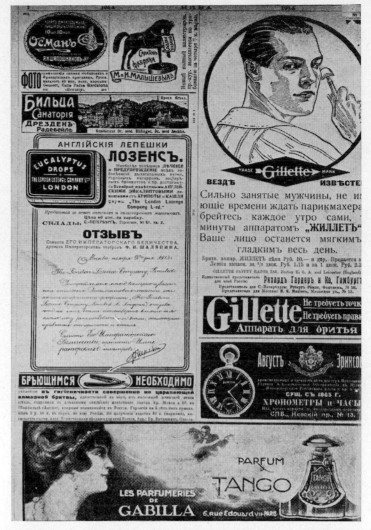

ILLUSTRATED weekly, *Niva*, was popular in the spring of 1914. Each month, its subscribers received one foreign and one Russian literary classic. It carried advertisements like these. (Gillette promises a three-minute shave which "leaves your skin soft and smooth all day.")

PROGRESS continues rapidly in Russia till 1914

The economic and social reforms which followed the Revolution of 1905 were accompanied by a general growth in Russia's intellectual life. The nation's leading scholars, scientists and writers continued to contribute to the older cultural magazines, and an excellent daily and weekly press was now reaching a large public throughout Russia. Pre-censorship of the press was abolished, and the newspapers gave complete coverage to world news, serialized contemporary literature, and published uncensored accounts of Duma debates. The opposition press reported in full the liberal and radical deputies' sharp questioning of Tsarist Ministers who tried to block reforms. Despite the Duma's limited powers (it had no control over the Tsar's appointment of ministers), it became an articulate voice of public opinion. While combatting the incompetence of the court and bureaucracy, as well as the inequities

which still existed, it gave the public a broad education in constitutional government. By 1914, autocracy had already become an anachronism in Russia.

BOLSHEVIK DAILY, *Pravda*, first appeared legally in 1912. Lenin wrote editorials from abroad; Stalin was briefly one of its editors. Masthead of its first issue is shown above.

PARIS was saved in September 1914, when General Galliéni's army rushed to the front in taxicabs and buses to help fight the Battle of the Marne. After this Allied victory, the German forces retreated. Their last major drive on the French capital came in March 1918.

SLOW WAR brings misery and graft, incenses the Tsar's last supporters

Progress in Russia came to an abrupt end with the outbreak of World War I. As it dragged on and on, the foundations of the Tsarist regime were gradually eaten away. Russian casualties were huge. There were increasing shortages of food, fuel and other necessities. Graft was exposed in war industries. A succession of incompetent ministers was appointed and dismissed on the whim of the Empress's favorite, the debauched monk Rasputin. The economy was dislocated by drafting fifteen million poorly equipped workers and peasants into the army. In Zimmerwald, Switzerland, in 1915, an international conference of Socialists had demanded an end to the conflict, but Lenin rejected this simple pacifist program. He wrote in a Party manifesto, "The only correct proletarian slogan is the transformation of the present imperialist war into a civil war." Despite hardships and discontent, the Russian army fought on, and in 1916 launched a great offensive under General Brusilov, timed to coincide with an Allied drive on the Somme. The Brusilov offensive took half a million prisoners, but further exhausted Russia. Suspicion of pro-German influence at the Court mounted; strikes multiplied with the rising cost of living. The dramatic assassination of Rasputin by incensed nobles in December 1916 was a clear indication that the Tsar and his consort had lost their last defenders.

RASPUTIN had great influence at the court because he could relieve the young Tsarevitch's haemophilia through hypnotism. The Empress

GALICIA was occupied by the Russians early in the war, but Austro-German forces struck back, re-entered the fortress of Przemysl (above) and moved into Poland. Russians remained on Austrian soil until the summer of 1917, when the Germans smashed their last push.

thought him holy and took his advice on policy, but she ignored his telegram warning that the war would mean "the end of all things."

STALIN, in Siberian exile, learned of Lenin's attitude toward the war from his neighbor Suren Spandarian (left). Lenin had sent Spandarian his *Theses*, which called for "turning the imperialist war into a civil war."

LENIN pushed his program on the war in a manifesto for the party newspaper *Sotsialdemokrat*, published in Geneva, November 1, 1914.

LITOVSKY CASTLE, HATED PRISON, WAS STORMED BY THE PEOPLE

FREEDOM comes to Russia when soldiers sent to break up hunger strikes turn their guns against the regime

PRINCE LVOV

Hunger touched off the democratic revolution of March 1917. On the 8th, Petrograd housewives pouring into the streets to demand bread were joined by 90,000 striking workers. The crowd increased to almost 200,000 the next day, and a Cossack squadron rode down the Nevsky Prospect without attempting to disperse it. Kerensky assailed the regime so strongly in the Duma that the Empress demanded he be hanged. On the 11th, some troops opened fire, but the Volinsky regiment, led by a sergeant, deserted its barracks on the 12th and joined the demonstration. When the soldiers marched to the Duma, Kerensky greeted them as "the first revolutionary guard." That day the Petrograd Soviet of Workers' and Soldiers' Deputies was organized, headed by Chkheidze, leader of the Social Democrats in the Duma, and Kerensky. On the 14th, Moscow rose. On the 15th, the Tsar abdicated, and an agreement between the Duma and the Soviet established a Provisional Government under Prince George Lvov, president of the Union of Zemstvos, with Kerensky as Minister of Justice. The new government released political prisoners; proclaimed freedom of speech, press and labor organizations; ended social, religious and ethnic restrictions; and promised to summon a Constituent Assembly to be elected by universal suffrage. The United States was the first to recognize it. President Wilson declared that "the great, generous Russian people have been added in all their naive majesty and might to the forces that are fighting for freedom in the world, for justice and peace."

ORDERED TO DISPERSE PETROGRAD CROWDS,

TSERETELLI (extreme right), the Social Democratic leader back from ten years' exile in Siberia, was the democratic Soviet's most forceful spokesman. He urged negotiations for a general peace without annexations or indemnities, but opposed a separate peace with Imperial Germany. To his right, Soviet chairman Chkheidze and Plekhanov.

BRESHKOVSKAYA, beloved "grandmother" of the revolution, returned from Siberia in triumph. "I do not think," she said, "there was ever a bride who received so many flowers."

THESE TROOPS JOINED THEM INSTEAD, FIRED ON THE POLITICAL PRISONS, OVERTHREW THE TSARIST AUTOCRACY AND BROUGHT FREEDOM TO RUSSIA

GENDARMES and agents of the Tsarist secret police were taken into custody (above) with little bloodshed. Among the Okhrana spies who were arrested was a former editor of the Bolshevik newspaper *Pravda*, Miron Chernomazov, with whom Stalin had worked briefly in 1912.

FUNERAL in Petrograd commemorated those who had died for freedom. In the huge procession was a Petrograd worker's daughter, 15-year-old Nadezhda Alliluyeva, whom Stalin married in 1919. Returning from exile on March 25, 1917, Stalin moved into the *Pravda* offices.

LUDENDORFF, German General Staff Chief, helped Lenin reach Russia. "Our government," he said, "in sending Lenin to Russia, took upon itself a tremendous responsibility. From a military viewpoint, his journey was justified, for it was imperative that Russia should fall."

BOLSHEVIK SAILORS of Kronstadt, the island fortress guarding Petrograd, took part in the uprising of July 17. Many civilians were killed in the street fighting (below, right). The sailors are shown (below, left) as they marched through the streets of Petrograd.

KERENSKY (center) succeeded Lvov as Premier and tried to rally the entire nation behind the government's war effort. In July, he or-

TRAPPED between Ludendorff

Foreign and internal enemies menaced the new democratic regime almost from its birth. Both the military clique in Imperial Germany and the Bolsheviks used the Russian desire for peace to subvert the Provisional Government, which remained loyal to Russia's allies. Berlin viewed Lenin's slogan of "turning the imperialist war into a civil war" as an effective way to eliminate Russia as a belligerent. With the approval of the Kaiser's

dered an offensive against Austro-German forces, to relieve the pressure on France. Its failure increased unrest, strengthened Lenin.

and Lenin, the new Russian democracy totters

General Staff, Lenin was allowed to travel in a sealed train through Germany. He arrived in Petrograd on April 16, 1917, after ten years' absence from Russia. He immediately called for peace, urging front-line soldiers to desert to their villages and seize land without waiting for an agrarian law. Trotsky, back from America, joined him and became the Soviet's star Bolshevik orator. In July, the Bolsheviks staged their first revolt.

DISGUISED (wig added, beard removed) Lenin fled to Finland to escape arrest after Bolshevik revolt in July. From his hideout he ordered preparations for another uprising.

MARIA BOCHKARIEVA (left), the wife of a peasant who had been killed in battle, headed the Women's Battalion of Death which fought against Germany in front-line trenches. Immune to Communist propaganda, the Women's Battalion strongly opposed a separate peace, and on November 7, 1917, it helped defend the Winter Palace, seat of the democratic government, against the Communist forces commanded by Antonov-Ovseenko. She is shown with Mrs. Emmeline Pankhurst, British feminist leader who had come to Russia in June.

GUNS from the cruiser *Aurora* helped these Communist forces seize the Winter Palace.

TROTSKY played the key role when the Bolsheviks took power. Stalin wrote in 1918 that the Petrograd coup occurred "under the direct leadership of . . . Comrade Trotsky."

DICTATORSHIP set up by Communist coup

pledges the people 'peace, bread and land' but destroys liberty

From July to October 1917, the Bolsheviks (who now began to call themselves "Communists") continued their "peace" drive, while inciting the peasants to seize the land. Impressed by Lenin's promises of immediate "peace, bread and land," the Petrograd garrison, mostly peasant sons, deserted the democratic government. On October 8, Trotsky became chairman of the Petrograd Soviet; the democratic leaders, Chkheidze, Tseretelli and Gotz, were forced out of the executive. Secretly, Lenin returned to Petrograd. On the 23rd, the Communist Central Committee voted to organize an immediate armed uprising. Lenin's forces—Kronstadt sailors, Lettish soldiers and Red Guards—captured the city on November 7, and that night formed a Communist regime called the "Council of People's Commissars." The next day, Trotsky's military committee, which had led the uprising, issued an order to the army which declared, "The program of the new government of the Petrograd Soviet consists in offering immediately a democratic peace, in transferring immediately the land of the large landowners to the peasants, in handing over all power to the Soviets, and in having an honest summoning of the Constituent Assembly." Within six weeks, the new regime ended freedom of the press, dispersed the All-Russian Peasants' Congress, dissolved the Petrograd and Moscow city councils, and established a secret police, called the Cheka, to crush all opposition by means of mass terror.

Отъ Военно - Революціоннаго Комитета при Петроградскомъ Совѣтѣ Рабочихъ и Солдатскихъ Депутатовъ.

Къ Гражданамъ Россіи.

Временное Правительство низложено. Государственная власть перешла въ руки органа Петроградскаго Совѣта Рабочихъ и Солдатскихъ Депутатовъ Военно-Революціоннаго Комитета, стоящаго во главѣ Петроградскаго пролетаріата и гарнизона.

Дѣло, за которое боролся народъ: немедленное предложеніе демократическаго мира, отмѣна помѣщичьей собственности на землю, рабочій контроль надъ производствомъ, созданіе Совѣтскаго Правительства — это дѣло обезпечено.

ДА ЗДРАВСТВУЕТЪ РЕВОЛЮЦІЯ РАБОЧИХЪ, СОЛДАТЪ И КРЕСТЬЯНЪ!

Военно-Революціонный Комитетъ
при Петроградскомъ Совѣтѣ
Рабочихъ и Солдатскихъ Депутатовъ.

25 октября 1917 г. 10 ч. утра.

FIRST DECREE of the Communists, signed by Trotsky's military committee, promised "a democratic peace, the abolition of landed estates, and workers' control of industry."

JOHN REED, an early American admirer of Communism, described the Bolshevik seizure of power in *Ten Days That Shook the World*, a book which Lenin praised highly. Stalin's name appears in it only once. Although Reed lies buried beneath the Kremlin, his book, translated into many languages, is now banned in the Soviet Union.

STALIN in 1917 was unknown to the public, but he was Commissar of Nationalities, a member of Lenin's Central Committee, and a vital cog in the Communist party machine.

KOKOSHKIN, scholar, member of democratic government and Constituent Assembly, was murdered in a hospital in 1918.

SHINGAREV, physician, Constituent Assembly deputy and member of democratic government, was killed with Kokoshkin.

SHCHEPKIN, a leading Constitutional Democrat in the Duma and the Zemstvos, was shot in Cheka headquarters in 1919.

ASTROV, a liberal, Russia's outstanding hydraulics expert, was shot with Shchepkin, despite Communist promises to free him.

TERROR starts as Lenin outlaws
liberals, arrests socialists, disperses parliament

The Communists seized power on November 7, 1917. Ten days later, a group of their leaders, headed by Alexei Rykov, Commissar of the Interior, and Leo Kamenev, chairman of the All-Russian Soviet Executive, resigned temporarily, charging that Lenin aimed at "the maintenance of a purely Bolshevik government by means of political terror." Most Russians rejected such a regime; in the elections for the Constituent Assembly on November 25, the Socialist Revolutionary Party polled over 20 million of the 36 million votes, the Communists only 9 million. Lenin struck back at once. On December 6, the members of the electoral commission were arrested; on the 11th, the Constitutional Democrats were outlawed; on the 31st, the Cheka ordered the arrest of Socialist Revolutionaries Victor Chernov and Abram Gotz, Social Democrat Tseretelli, and other democratic leaders. Most of them remained in hiding until the Assembly met in the Tauride Palace on January 18. Although armed Communist sailors and Lettish guards occupied gallery seats, the Assembly elected Chernov president and tried to go about its business. With rifles pointed at his head, Tseretelli warned that the dictatorship was bringing civil war. The next day, machine guns barred the palace entrance. In protest, Lenin's friend Maxim Gorky wrote, "For nearly a century the best of the Russians . . . visualized the Constituent Assembly as a political organ capable of giving Russian democracy an opportunity of freely expressing its will. . . . Rivers of blood have been shed for this sacred idea. And now that this goal has been reached, and the democracy has come out to rejoice, the 'People's Commissars' have given orders to shoot. . . . I ask the 'People's Commissars,' among whom there should be honest and sensible men, if they understand that . . . they are crushing the Russian democracy, destroying the conquests of the revolution?"

KRONSTADT sailors and Red Guards fired on the crowds supporting the Constituent Assembly, helped Lenin disperse it.

FELIX DZERZHINSKY, the son of a rich Polish landowner, was named on December 20, 1917 to set up the Cheka, Communist secret police later known as the GPU and NKVD, and now as the MVD. In his first address as its chief, Dzerzhinsky said, "Do not think I am on the lookout for forms of revolutionary justice. We have no need of justice now. Now we need a battle to the death." In 1918, he selected the present central headquarters of the Soviet secret police, the former offices of an insurance company at 22 Lubianka Street, Moscow.

BREST-LITOVSK treaty, March 1918, was not the "democratic peace" Lenin had promised. It gave the Baltic and Ukraine regions to Imperial Germany, stripped Russia of most of its coal and iron, and ceded the Batum oil fields to Turkey. Trotsky (center), the chief Soviet negotiator, opposed it, and vainly tried to stir a Communist revolt in the German army; but Communist "peace" propaganda had disintegrated Russia's front-line troops, and Lenin had to sign. The treaty was nullified by the Allied victory eight months later.

CZECH LEGION valiantly fought the Germans in the Ukraine after Brest-Litovsk and was officially commended by the Soviets for its "brotherly aid . . . in the struggle of the laboring people against the hordes of base imperialism." The Czechs then asked to sail from Vladivostok to serve on the Western front. The Soviets agreed to give them unobstructed passage across Siberia, but after a Czech-Soviet clash in the Urals, the Legion joined forces with democratic Russian elements and held the Communists troops at bay for months.

STALIN wired from Tsaritsyn a pledge of "open mass systematic terror against the bourgeoisie and its agents" on hearing of a woman revolutionist's attempt to kill Lenin.

22-го сентября 1918 года.

PROTEST against drafting engineers planning a Volga-Don Canal drew this reply in Stalin's handwriting, "We'll dig the canal after we have drowned the Constitutional Democrats in the Volga and the Don" (Sept. 20, 1918). Voroshilov added his signature to Stalin's.

CIVIL WAR engulfs Russia
when volunteer armies fight Communist rule

Lenin was entrenched in Petrograd and Moscow (which again became the capital in 1918), but large areas resisted Communist rule. In Siberia and Central Russia, Socialist Revolutionary deputies of the Constituent Assembly organized a people's army, aided by the Czech Legion in Russia, which had deserted the Austro-Hungarian army to fight on the Allied side. The Czechs, ordered to surrender their arms, revolted in May 1918, joined the Socialist Revolutionaries, and seized parts of Siberia and the Volga region. In the Don area, former commanding generals of the Russian army recruited a volunteer force. Meanwhile, Trotsky, who had become War Commissar, was organizing a Red Army. He staffed it with conscripted Tsarist officers and placed Communist commissars at their side. By September 1918, the Red Army was on the offensive; in November, the anti-Communist government in Siberia, led by Constituent Assembly deputies, was ousted by Admiral Kolchak. Democratic forces were caught between Trotsky's Red Army and Kolchak's "Whites."

SHOOTING of peasants was shown in *Two Years of Struggle on the Internal Front* by M. Y. Latsis, deputy chief of the Cheka, who says "The picture shows mutilated Communists. Our unit is already on the scene of the crime and is about to execute the rebel leaders."

FUNERAL of Plekhanov (Petrograd, June 1918) became an anti-Communist labor demonstration when, despite a posted edict banning a parade, workers from many cities (above, from Moscow) marched. The founder of Marxism in Russia died a bitter foe of the regime.

TCHAIKOVSKY (right), The People's Socialist, head of the Archangel government (1918), resigned when a British general dictated policy. At left, U. S. envoy David Francis.

INTERVENTION by Allies

with differing aims plays into Lenin's hands

Although Allied intervention during the Russian civil war began with the effort to restore an eastern front against Germany, it soon reflected conflicting aims. On January 8, 1918, President Wilson declared that "the treatment accorded Russia by her sister nations in the months to come will be the acid test of their goodwill, of their comprehension of her needs as distinguished from their own interests, and of their intelligent and unselfish sympathy." To this principle the United States adhered more closely than any other Allied power. Food and medical aid supplied to famine areas by the American Red Cross and American Relief Administration saved thousands of Russian lives. American troops who landed in Archangel in August, 1918, did not interfere in the local government and took little part in the fighting, and American troops sent to Vladivostok to expedite the transport of the Czech Legion helped frustrate Japan's ambition to carve out a buffer state from the Pacific to Lake Baikal. Japan's 70,000 troops in Eastern Siberia were supporting reactionary soldiers of fortune against local democratic elements who governed a Far Eastern Republic until 1922. Japan's policy, strongly opposed by the United States, operated to the Kremlin's advantage, as the local population came to resent foreign rule. Great Britain and France were motivated more by commercial interest than by the desire to meet Wilson's "acid test." On December 17, 1917, an Anglo-French agreement defined the Cossack region, Armenia, Georgia and Kurdistan as the British "zone of influence," while the French sphere was Bessarabia, the Ukraine and Crimea. After the armistice, the British occupied the Caucasian oil fields. These moves did more to persuade patriotic Russian officers to serve in the Red Army than did Cheka machine guns and political commissars. With prophetic clarity, Winston Churchill opposed both the Communist dictatorship and the short-range Anglo-French policy. On July 21, 1919, he warned the world, "Russia, like all great nations, is indestructible. Either she must continue to suffer and her sufferings will disturb and convulse the whole world, or she must be rescued. . . . I say to the thoughtless, I say to the uninstructed, I say to the simple, I say to the busy—you may abandon Russia, but Russia will not abandon you. . . . You cannot remake the world without Russia. You cannot go on into victory and prosperity and peace and leave that vast proportion of the human race suffering torture in the night of barbarism. I appeal to those who have the future peace of the world at heart . . . to take a grand view of the whole position of Russia, and to make one united, concerted effort to deliver the Russian nation from her appalling fate and to restore peace to the tortured world." No one heeded.

FOOD was supplied to the population of Murmansk in North Russia by treaty between the United States, Britain and France, and the local authorities. Rations were also dispatched to Archangel. At the school above, an American Red Cross team serves lunch to children.

MEDICAL AID donated by American relief organizations on many Russian civil war fronts combatted the epidemics which resulted from widespread famine. Dental care was also provided. Above, the staff of a mobile clinic beside its eight-car Red Cross dental train.

ARMISTICE (November 11, 1918) was greeted by joyous crowds in New York (above), London and Paris. To millions, the end of the fighting on the western front spelled peace and a return to normalcy. In Russia, meanwhile, new millions were perishing in the civil war.

WOODROW WILSON sailed for France on December 4, 1918, to fight for the Covenant of the League of Nations. When his hopes for a democratic world were shattered by European power politics and American isolationism, he predicted new conflicts in which "not a few hundred thousand fine men from America will have to die, but as many millions as are necessary to accomplish the final freedom of the peoples of the world." The young man in the top hat at left is Wilson's Assistant Secretary of the Navy, Franklin D. Roosevelt.

CONQUEST of independent Georgia was led by Stalin's deputies, Kirov and Ordzhonikidze (second and third from left). Ordzhonikidze commanded the Second Red Army. Kirov was nominally the Kremlin's ambassador to the Georgian Republic, but a recent Soviet history de-

KRONSTADT sailors, called "the pride and glory of the Bolshevik revolution," had demonstrated for "All Power to the Soviets" in 1917 (above); but in 1921 they rose against Lenin, demanding the restoration of political freedom and an end to the misery shown below.

MORE TERROR mows

A few months after the last White forces were defeated, new revolts expressed the popular protest against wretched living conditions and the loss of freedom. Three years of Communism had brought Russia to the brink of economic collapse—her industry almost at a standstill, unemployment widespread, the harvest only 37 per cent of normal, the barest necessities unobtainable. In Central Russia, peasants rose against the Cheka's seizures of their grain. In Petrograd, illegal proclamations appeared on the city walls: "Workers and peasants need freedom. They don't want to live by Bolshevik decrees. They want to control their own destiny." When the hungry workers struck against special food rations for Communist officials, Zinoviev sent machine guns to disperse them. The unrest quickly spread to nearby Kronstadt; on March 1, 1921, some 16,000 sailors, soldiers and workers in the citadel elected a revolutionary committee and demanded freedom of speech, press and trade union organization, elections by secret ballot, abolition of political commissars in the army, an end to forcible grain requisitions, and a free market for peasants. To silence Kronstadt, whose sailors had carried the Bolsheviks to power three years before, Lenin now sent Trotsky and General Tukhachevsky, a former Tsarist officer, with 60,000 Cheka and other crack forces. The sailors replied, "Here is raised the banner of rebellion against the three-year-old tyranny and oppression of Communist autoc-

clares that he was "leading the Bolshevik organizations in Georgia." The bearded man in the fur hat (right) is Mikoyan. All three of them looked to Stalin for leadership, and were climbing with him in the party organization. This picture was taken in 1921, in Baku.

down sailors' revolt and smashes free Georgia

racy which has put in the shade the three-hundred-year-old despotism of monarchy." Communist troops attacked across the ice of the Finnish Gulf and fought the sailors hand to hand. On March 17, an observer wrote, "Kronstadt has fallen today. Thousands of sailors and workers lie dead in its streets. Summary execution of prisoners and hostages continues." A few hundred sailors managed to escape to Finland to tell their story. While the Cheka was mopping up Kronstadt, it suppressed a Red Army mutiny in nearby Oranienbaum. Meanwhile, on February 11, Stalin had issued an order on his sole responsibility—the Politburo did not confirm it until three days later: the Second Red Army was to invade his native Georgia. Georgia had become independent in 1918 under a democratic socialist government, headed by Stalin's first teacher, Noah Jordania, and Nicholas Chkheidze, former chairman of the Petrograd Soviet. The Kremlin, nine months before, had guaranteed its integrity by a treaty, on the strength of which Britain ended her 20-month occupation and withdrew her forces. The invasion proceeded; Tiflis, the capital, fell on February 25, and a Communist regime was installed, headed by Philip Makharadze, a moderate. In July, Stalin paid his first visit to Georgia since 1912, and reorganized the local Cheka and Party command. A year later, the Red Army had to use armor to put down new uprisings in Tiflis and peasant districts. Despite these stern measures, unrest continued.

FOOD and clothing began to appear in Russian stores (like the Moscow shop above) soon after the New Economy Policy put an end to "war communism" and restored private trade. Real wages for Russian workers reached their all-time Soviet high during the NEP.

TRADE in open markets flourished during this liberal period. Co-operatives were allowed to purchase farm produce and lease industrial enterprises. Artisans could buy raw materials and sell the finished products. "Communists," said Lenin, "must learn to trade."

NEP allows private trade, helps the farmers and gives the workers more food

Lenin knew that the strikes, the peasant revolts, and the Kronstadt uprising spelled danger to the Soviet regime. While the Kronstadt battle still raged, he told the Tenth Party Congress on March 15, 1921 that "we must try to satisfy the demands of the peasants." He halted grain seizures, allowed peasants to sell their produce in the open market, and authorized the private manufacture and sale of consumers' goods. That October, he admitted that "the system of distribution in the villages and the immediate application of Communist methods in the towns held back our productive forces and caused the great economic and political crisis we met in the spring of 1921." Under his New Economic Policy (NEP), conditions improved in the cities and countryside. Still, Lenin not only rejected popular demands for political liberty, but turned down the request of oppositionists on the Central Committee for greater freedom of discussion inside the party. "Terror cannot be dispensed with," he wrote, "notwithstanding the hypocrites and phrase-mongers." The ironclad dictatorship of the Politburo silenced criticism.

INVALIDED by a stroke in 1922, Lenin began to question much of what the Communist regime had done. When some Party leaders urged that farm lands be collectivized, he replied: "The question of collective farms is not on the order of the day. . . . The transformation of the peasant's psychology and habits is something that requires generations. The use of force will not help." He now defined socialism as "an order of civilized cooperators in which the means of production are socially owned." With him is Krupskaya, his wife.

FASCISTS promise 'protection'
to the industrialists and ape the Communists

Although by 1922 the Communist drive had largely spent itself in Western Europe, a new enemy was striking against liberty. In Germany and Italy, many industrialists, officers and landowners used the specter of social revolution as an excuse for assaulting republican institutions. Generals like Ludendorff, who refused responsibility for the 1918 defeat, claimed that Germany had been "stabbed in the back" by civilians. Their campaign incited nationalists to murder two leading democratic statesmen, Erzberger (1921) and Rathenau (1922). The German military clique also flouted the Versailles Treaty by making a secret deal with the Kremlin in 1921 to permit their training in Russia with forbidden weapons (planes, heavy artillery, gas, tanks), while giving instruction to Red Army officers. Deputies who exposed the pact in the Reichstag were branded as "traitors." In Munich the disgruntled elements had turned to a Reichswehr informer named Adolf Hitler, who was making fervid speeches in local taverns against France, the Versailles Treaty and "international Jewry." A newspaper said of his first mass meeting, in 1920, "Hitler expounded some striking political ideas." In Italy, an ex-radical journalist, Benito Mussolini, was winning financial support for his party by promising to restore Roman grandeur to the debt-ridden nation. Meanwhile, his Black Shirt squads were driving workers from factories they had seized in strikes after the war. The name of liberty's new enemy was fascism.

MARCH on Rome made Mussolini dictator of Italy on October 27, 1922. Less than a year later, he bombarded the Greek island of Corfu and occupied it for a month until Great Britain forced him to withdraw. After his Black Shirts murdered the Socialist leader Giacomo Matteotti on June 10, 1924, Mussolini quelled disturbances by jailings and by exiling his opponents to the Lipari Islands.

INFLATION in 1923 hit German workers and small businessmen hardest. The five million mark note above was worthless paper.

PLOT by Hitler and (in center) Ludendorff to seize power in Munich was beaten down by government troops on November 9, 1923. When Hitler was released from prison, after serving less than a year of his five-year term, he had written *Mein Kampf.* Second from right is the head of his Storm Troops, Captain Roehm, whom he executed with other former comrades in the purge of 1934.

PERNET   Dr. WEBER   FRICK   KRIEBEL   LUDENDORFF

When
few Ru
before.
Politbu
he hac
in his
rade S
enorme
knows
4, he
entirel
insupp
propos
that p
spects
patient
rades,
even n
of Wo
Stalin.
missar
at the
a mor
Peasar
nothin
he dict
relatio
Makh
since
the co
Lenin
invalic
Zinovi
Trotsk
had he
Lenin
monies
mausо

MILLION DOLLAR gate at Dempsey-Carpentier fight at Boyle's Thirty Acres (July 2, 1921) was a highlight of the Roaring Twenties. Wages were good, taxes low; the country steered clear of European quarrels. Dempsey won by a knockout in the fourth round to keep title.

PRESIDING JUDGE PIATAKOV READS DEATH SENTENCE TO THE SOCIALISTS

THE FIRST MOSCOW TRIAL

On June 8, 1922, twelve Socialist Revolutionary leaders went on trial in Moscow. The accused had spent years in Tsarist prisons; Abram Gotz, the leading figure, had been sentenced to death in 1907. Defense lawyers from outside, including Theodore Liebknecht, brother of the slain German Communist, were permitted at first, but were soon forced to withdraw. When the defendants protested, Judge Yuri Piatakov said that the Soviet court "laughs at the hypocritical assertions of bourgeois countries that courts must stand above classes and render verdicts of some sort of supernatural impartiality." At the last moment, the court offered to release the accused if they "repented." The defendant Eugene Timoteyev replied: "There can be no question of repentance or disavowal. From these benches you will never hear anything like that." After the twelve had been condemned to death, the Kremlin announced that they would be held in prison as permanent hostages, to be executed in the event of a new uprising.

LAST R
Kamer
abroad
For a

HITLER BRÜCKNER RÖHM WAGNER

LENIN'S SUCCESSORS take a promenade in Moscow. Alexei Rykov (second from the left) succeeded him as Premier; the triumvirate of Stalin, Leo Kamenev (pointing) and Gregory Zinoviev ruled the Party.

STALIN outsmarts all his rivals and succeeds Lenin as dictator

With Lenin gone, Stalin soon demonstrated his skill as a machine politician. He encouraged Zinoviev and Kamenev, who ran the Leningrad and Moscow Party organizations, to dig out and publicize Trotsky's "sins" before he had joined the Bolsheviks. In November 1924, Stalin himself reminded the Central Council of Trade Unions that Trotsky had written in 1913, "The whole structure of Leninism is at present based on lies and falsifications and harbors the germs of its own decomposition." He charged that Trotsky was "too fond of terror" and that his proposal to collectivize Russia's 25 million farm households would mean "the proclamation of civil war in our country." He compared Trotsky's program for building heavy industries to a peasant's buying a gramophone instead of a cow. Stalin's attack on Trotsky's radicalism won him support in Party organizations throughout the country. In the Politburo, it won the approval of Premier Rykov,

trade union chief Tomsky, and Party theoretician Bukharin, all of whom advocated restoring Russia to economic health by aiding the individual farmer and by manufacturing consumers' goods. The campaign against Trotsky led to his removal as War Commissar in January 1925. Zinoviev and Kamenev belatedly joined him in a "Left Opposition" to Stalin, but they were defeated and expelled from the Party in November 1927. Stalin now reversed himself and convinced the Party machine that the Rykov-Tomsky-Bukharin program of light industry and farm aid would lead to the overthrow of Communist rule by the "bourgeois" farmers. By the end of 1929, Trotsky's collectivization-industrialization program was well under way as the first "Stalin Five Year Plan." Rykov, Tomsky and Bukharin were forced to recant their "Rightist deviations." On Stalin's fiftieth birthday, December 21, 1929, the Soviet press proclaimed, "Stalin is the Lenin of today."

STORY OF THE UNEXTINGUISHED MOON

◄ Mikhail Frunze (extreme left) suppressed a new rebellion in Georgia in August 1924, with assistance from Ordzhonikidze (fur cap). In January 1925, Frunze replaced Trotsky as War Commissar, but died of an operation the same year. Rumor said that Kremlin doctors had ruled the operation unnecessary, but that Stalin had ordered Frunze to go through with it. Some time later, the Moscow literary review *Krasnaya Nov* printed Boris Pilnyak's *Story of the Unextinguished Moon: The Assassination of the Commandant*, which publicized this rumor. Stalin had the copies of the issue confiscated. Pilnyak vanished, under arrest. Voroshilov succeeded Frunze as War Commissar.

AUTHOR PILNYAK

"LIQUIDATION of the Kulaks" was Stalin's 1929 slogan, displayed on banner above. His 1933 slogan: "To recruit real, tried Bolshevik cadres for the collective farms and to make them really Bolshevik collective farms." The Party controlled the farms through machine tractor stations which acted as nerve centers for many collectives.

OUSTED as Premier in 1930, Rykov had favored giving the peasants modern tools, paying higher grain prices, producing consumers' goods to raise living standards.

OFFICIAL composite photo shows President Kalinin deeding the land of the peasants to a collective farm, as peasants in Kazakstan stand beneath a banner which heralds the promise of a far better life "under the leadership of the genius Stalin."

SUDDEN death of Alliluyeva (left), Stalin's young wife, in 1932 is reported to have followed a quarrel with him at a party at Voroshilov's, where she blamed collectivization for famine. Above, her head in marble, in convent graveyard.

DEATH reaps the harvest as Stalin takes the land
from peasants, uproots millions and imposes collective serfdom

Compulsory collectivization of Russia's farms began on December 27, 1929, when Stalin ordered "the liquidation of the kulaks as a class." Kulaks were peasants who had become self-sufficient under the New Economic Policy. Soviet figures listed 5,618,000 of them in 1928. In 1934, only 149,000 remained; some five million of the rest had been deported to forced labor camps. With farmlands under its control, the regime could export grain to buy machine tools. However, the main reason for collectivization was political; on January 18, 1930, *Leningrad Pravda* declared that "as long as agriculture was developed on the basis of small, individual bourgeois farms, the

existence of the proletarian dictatorship was endangered." Rebellious peasants battled GPU troops, but when word of this caused Red Army rumblings, Stalin blamed his subordinates for growing "dizzy with success" and condemned the "cavalry raids" against the villages. Between 1929 and 1933, collectivization cost Russia more than half her livestock; and in addition to the five million kulak deportees, another five million people died in the ensuing famine of 1932-33. By 1938, nine-tenths of the farms were party-directed collectives. Stalin later told Churchill that collectivization was worse than World War II and admitted that it had involved ten million lives.

SATISFIED with the effectiveness of his policy of strengthening Communist power by crushing all the independent farmers, Stalin scoffed at the critics who advocated caution, "You do not lament the loss of hair of one who has been beheaded."

LABOR builds blast furnaces, canals, power dams and cities, but loses its rights

Under Stalin's First Five Year Plan (1928-1932), giant new iron and coal mines were developed in the Urals and Siberia; new blast furnaces, automotive plants, power dams and canals were rapidly constructed; the urban population, which was 28,000,-000 in 1929, increased to 56,000,000 within ten years. To pay in hard foreign currency for tools and dies, as well as for the services of British, German and American engineers, peasants herded to the frozen forests of North Russia hewed timber for export, while the collective farms delivered their grain to foreign markets. The construction program made severe demands on labor. An American who worked on the Magnitogorsk project wrote, "I would wager that Russia's battle of ferrous metallurgy alone involved more lives than the Battle of the Marne." Meanwhile, the secret police (called the GPU in this phase) was no longer merely an instrument of political terror. Under its new chief, Henry Yagoda, it had become a great contractor of forced labor. In the construction of the Baltic-White Sea canal, for instance, the GPU employed several hundred thousand exiled peasants, as well as disaffected engineers and others. The Stalin construction program also completely transformed labor relations. It introduced work books, recording absence and lateness; penalties were stiff. Workers could no longer change jobs with-

out official permission. The weekly wage was replaced by the piece-work system; large bonuses were paid to shock workers who paced the output. A 1934 study showed that the new elite workers were earning 28.3 times as much as the lowest paid. For most Russian workers, real wages declined steadily. In 1937, steel output was four times as high as in 1913, but workers ate less butter, eggs and meat than before the war and under the New Economic Policy. Oil output was three times higher than in 1913, but workers had only one-third as much tea for their samovars. In 1912, Russia had 1,166,000 department stores, wholesale units and retail stores to meet consumers' needs; in October 1937, there were only 228,000 distribution stores and 98,000 warehouses. To meet the high living costs, housewives entered factories on an unprecedented scale. In the twenties, only 28 per cent of industrial workers were women; in 1935, they constituted 38 per cent. Since industrial expansion was not matched by housing, workers had less living space—4.3 square meters per person in 1937, as compared with 8 in 1913. In 1934, Stalin replied to charges that the Soviet Union was a new class society by remarking that the idea of social equality was "a reactionary petty bourgeois absurdity worthy of a primitive sect of ascetics, but not of a socialist society on Marxian lines."

←LABOR moved into new heavy industry before factory buildings were finished (left, mess hall of new auto plant, Jan. 1931). In 1933, collective bargaining was abolished.

LIMOUSINES for the upper-income bracket of Soviet society were assembled in the Stalin Automobile Works, Moscow. Above, Stalin inspects windshield wiper on a new model.

FAILURE of the First Five Year Plan to benefit the ordinary citizen was officially blamed on the sabotage of British engineers in the Moscow trial of March 1933. Above, Judge Ulrich (foreground) reads the verdict. Standing at his right, Prosecutor Andrei Vishinsky.

PACERS like former miner Alexei Stakhanov (above) steadily raised the norms which labor had to meet under the piece-work system. The "Stakhanovites" received government and Party jobs. By 1934, only 9.3 per cent of Communists were workers, compared to 48.6 in 1930.

CRASH on the New York Stock Exchange in October 1929 wiped out some thirty billion dollars of inflated values in a few weeks. It set off a depression that cut U. S. production in half within three years, closed 2,298 banks in 1931 alone, and engulfed all of Europe.

UNEMPLOYED in the United States numbered 3,000,000 by 1930, and totals kept rising. Labor's 1929 income shrank 50 per cent in four years; in 1933, the average factory worker earned only $16.73 a week. The song of the day was "Brother, Can You Spare a Dime?"

INDEPENDENT American Communist, Benjamin Gitlow, defied Stalin in Moscow. He was forced out of Party leadership although most U. S. Communists supported him.

CRASH floors Wall Street, shuts factories and banks, boosts J. V. Stalin's stock

Admiration for Soviet planned economy gained vast ground when a worldwide depression followed the Wall Street crash of 1929. Anticipating the crisis, the Sixth Comintern Congress in 1928 ordered an all-out fight against "reformist" unions and socialists as allies of "moribund capitalism." The Comintern instructed its members to utilize workers' "minor, everyday needs as a starting point from which to lead the working class to the revolutionary struggle for power." The Party was to engage in "a combination of strikes and demonstrations; a combination of strikes and *armed* demonstrations; and finally, the general strike conjointly with armed insurrection against the State power of the bourgeoisie." As unemployment spread, the Communists followed Moscow's instructions, organized "hunger marches" and "unemployed councils," and presented Stalin's planned economy in glowing colors. In the United States and Europe, many thoughtful citizens of all classes decided that the Soviet state, despite its rigors, represented the wave of the future. And in Germany, the depression enabled Adolf Hitler's Nazi Party, which had held only 12 seats in the 1928 Reichstag, to poll six million votes and elect 107 deputies in September 1930. "It is not for seats in Parliament that we fight," blared Hitler two days after the election, "but we win seats in Parliament in order that one day we may be able to liberate the German people."

COMMUNISTS exploited the depression by demonstrating for relief (parade in St. Louis above), leading a veterans' bonus march on Washington, and solemnly contrasting Stalinist production with the American economic crisis. This last impressed many intellectuals.

CONFIDENT that capitalism would destroy itself, Stalin adopted a hard revolutionary line before the depression. On November 7, 1927, he declared, "The era of the 'stabilization' of capitalism has gone, taking along with it the legend of the unshakable character of the bourgeois order. The era of the downfall of capitalism has begun." Bukharin (center), head of the Comintern, who had thought that Western economies were temporarily secure, was routed by Stalin at the Sixth Comintern Congress in 1928. At right, Ordzhonikidze.

BERNARD SHAW said, "A considerable share of the secret of the success of Russian Communism consists in the fact that every Russian knows that if he will not make his life a paying enterprise for his country, then he will most likely lose it. An agent of the GPU will take him by the shoulder and will conduct him to the cellar of this famous department and he will simply stop living." *Pravda* printed his remarks without comment on May 13, 1932. Lady Astor is at his right in this Moscow photo. Extreme left, Party writer Radek.

59

VIRTUOSO of modulated Communist themes, Willi Muenzenberg influenced millions through first great network of "front organizations," "innocent" magazines, newspapers, film company, book club. "We have to organize the intellectuals," he informed the Party.

SOCIALISTS stamped their three-arrowed emblem over the Nazis' swastika and organized the republican "Reichsbanner" to fight Storm Troopers. Members of the Reichsbanner, holding a captured Nazi flag, are shown during an election in Berlin.

MAIN ENEMY in Germany, said Stalin (shown in his Kremlin office), was the Social Democratic Party. The "right road" for Communists, he said in June 1930, was "waging an irreconcilable struggle against Social Democracy." A picture of Karl Marx hangs above his head.

COMMUNISTS aim blows
at the German Socialists, scoff at Nazi threat

In October 1931, Hitler concluded a political alliance with Dr. Hugenberg, head of the German Nationalist Party. Industrial barons like Thyssen and Krupp von Bohlen poured money into Nazi coffers to pay for newspapers, Storm Troop uniforms and equipment, and impressive parades against the republic. With six million German workers on the dole and strident nationalism on the march, the survival of German freedom depended on organized labor and liberal elements in the Catholic Centrist Party. The German Communist Party, which polled five million votes, held the balance of power. Catholic workers and Social Democrats appealed for a united stand against the Nazis, but *Pravda* said on November 6, 1931, "The main task of the German Communist Party is to expose the maneuvers of the Social Democracy, its attempts to deceive the masses with slogans of 'freedom,' 'democracy,' 'socialism,' 'control of the banks,' 'state socialism,' etc. The Communist parties are conducting and will continue to conduct an unceasing day to day struggle against the whole Social Democracy. . . . Only by conducting a battle of extermination against the Social Democracy can one fight fascism." On November 17, the official organ of the German Communist Party, *Rote Fahne*, proclaimed, "Social Democracy is our main enemy in the proletariat. Against Social Democracy we carry on our main fight in the present period of the class struggle." The Comintern agreed with Stalin's dictum that Fascism and Social Democracy "do not contradict but supplement one another. They are not antipodes but twins."

COCKSURE German Communist leader Ernst Thaelmann (left, wearing Red Front uniform and giving its clenched-fist salute) said on November 19, 1932 that "nothing would be more fatal than an opportunist over-estimation of Hitlerite Fascism. . . . It would be false to believe that the most important process that is taking place in Germany at present is the growth of Fascism." When he ran for President in March 1932, republicans were forced to support Hindenburg against Hitler. Thaelmann died in a Nazi concentration camp in 1945.

BLINDED by the anti-democratic campaign of their leaders, Berlin Communist workers still clamored "For the Dictatorship of the Proletariat" (on front banner above) only a few months before Hitler took power. Their anti-Hitler cartoons failed to alarm the Nazis.

JOINT STRIKE against the Berlin transit system by the Communists and Nazis in November 1932 helped undermine the crumbling republic, gave the public another argument for a "strong" government. Above, pickets at a subway station in the heart of metropolitan Berlin.

STORM TROOPERS marched against the Karl Liebknecht House, Communist headquarters in Berlin, on January 22, 1933, as the Communist policy of united front with the Nazis boomeranged. Pictures of Lenin, Liebknecht and Rosa Luxemburg adorn the building.

TRIPLE PLAY by the Nazis,

President von Hindenburg ousted Catholic Premier Bruening in May 1932 and replaced him with Franz von Papen, a World War I espionage agent. A few days later, a motion of non-confidence in the Social Democratic government of Prussia, introduced by Communist Wilhelm Pieck, was carried by the combined vote of Communists, Nationalists and Nazis, and soon afterwards von Papen dispersed the Prussian government, thereby taking the Prussian police out of republican hands. In July, the Communist Central Committee said that to unite with the Social Democratic unions against Hitler would "only disarm the proletariat." On January 30, 1933, Hitler became Chancellor and von Papen

UNRUFFLED German Red chieftain Fritz Heckert (above) remained confident of ultimate Communist success in Germany. He wrote in 1933 that "the jailing of a few thousand Communists cannot kill a party with a following of about five millions." Heckert fled to Moscow.

ANGERED German Communist Heinz Neumann blamed his own party's policies for the Nazi victory. The Comintern replied that "the views of Neumann and his group . . . constitute an open attack . . . upon Comrades Stalin and [then Comintern leader] Manuilsky."

◀ **MOCK REVERENCE** toward conservative President von Hindenburg cloaked Hitler's swift moves to oust his non-Nazi allies.

PUBLIC INSULTS to Jews (above) began as soon as the Nazis took power. Anti-Semitic laws and party-led pogroms followed.

Nationalists and Communists wins for Hitler

Vice-Chancellor in a Nazi-Nationalist coalition cabinet. On March 23, the Reichstag voted Hitler dictatorial powers for four years. On May 2, the Nazi Labor Front seized the trade unions. On May 10, books were publicly burned in Berlin. None of this perturbed Stalin. On January 26, 1934, he denied that fascism was a bar to good relations with Hitler's Reich, "if only for the reason that fascism in Italy, for example, has not prevented the U.S.S.R. from establishing the best relations with that country." In the same address, however, he expressed concern over a speech in London by Hitler's Finance Minister Hugenberg, which suggested that Germany be given a free hand in the Ukraine.

PACT for five-year Franco-Soviet alliance was concluded by Stalin and French Foreign Minister Pierre Laval on May 2, 1934. Four years earlier, Stalin had described France as "the most aggressive and militarist country of all aggressive and militarist countries of the world." When Laval returned to Paris, he said that Stalin had authorized him to say that he sympathized with France's effort to strengthen its defenses. On May 16, 1934, Stalin also signed a pact with Czechoslovakia, represented by Foreign Minister Eduard Benes.

GENERAL STAFF of the Comintern at its Seventh Congress. Front, from left: Bulgaria's Georgi Dimitrov; Italy's Palmiro Togliatti; Germany's Wilhelm Florin; China's Chen Shao-yo (Wang Ming). Rear: Finland's Otto Kuusinen; Czechoslovakia's Klement Gottwald; Germany's Wilhelm Pieck; Stalin's personal deputy, Dmitri Manuilsky. Dimitrov, whose defiance of Goering at the Reichstag fire trial made him an anti-fascist symbol, became Comintern leader in place of Manuilsky, who had been denouncing Social Democrats bitterly.

TROJAN HORSE returns to open Western strongholds to the Communists

When it became clear that Hitler had large designs in the East, Stalin changed his tactics. He not only joined the League of Nations and signed pacts with France and Czechoslovakia; he suddenly introduced what seemed to be a radical shift in the policy of the Communist International. The new line was officially inaugurated at the Comintern's Seventh Congress, held in Moscow from July 25 to August 20, 1935, with Georgi Dimitrov, the Bulgarian Communist leader, as its spokesman. The Congress instructed Communist parties abroad to work for "popular fronts" with liberal and socialist elements who opposed Hitler. Party leaders were cautioned not to frighten away middle-class groups with anticapitalist slogans and were ordered to support rearmament, to collaborate with non-Communists in trade unions, and to discontinue open attacks on parliamentary institutions. Overnight, Communists throughout the world dropped their assaults on the League of Nations, "Anglo-French imperialism," social democracy and "reformist" trade unions. In Europe and America, the new line was widely interpreted by non-Communists as Stalin's renunciation of Communist world revolution. But Dimitrov had also told the Comintern, "Patiently, step by step, we must make it easier for the broad masses to come over to the positions of Communism"; he had recalled the conquest of Troy and advised Communists to get "into the heart of the enemy with the help of the Trojan horse"; and the Congress restated Communism's aims: "The establishment of the united front of the working class is the decisive link in the preparation of the toilers for the forthcoming great battles of the second round of proletarian revolution."

MILITARY envoy of Stalin, Marshal Mikhail Tukhachevsky (shown leaving a War Ministry session in Paris), was sent to France in 1936 to confer with her top military men.

VIOLENCE in labor disputes was seized on by skilled U. S. Communists to acquire key posts in labor-management relations. Above, striking Republic Steel workers battle South Chicago police, March 31, 1937; most steel magnates had recognized their union, but Republic's Tom Girdler held out. Experienced organizers, some Comintern-trained, moved into previously unorganized strategic industries; lawyers who concealed their Communist affiliations were active in the National Labor Relations Board. Older unions established broad educational

INTELLECTUAL Romain Rolland (rear, with French Communist Jacques Duclos) wrote, "People must be led to their own happiness against their own will," and backed Stalin.

CLERGYMAN Hewlett Johnson, the Dean of Canterbury, toured the U.S.S.R. and found "a new form of democracy" marked by "complete equality" and "absence of fear."

SCHOLARS Sidney and Beatrice Webb brought out their two-volume, 1200-page work entitled *Soviet Communism, a New Civilization?* in 1936. With a multitude of footnotes

FRONT MEN cheer Stalin,

befuddle West, drown out truth about Russia

During the popular front era (July 1935-August 1939), Stalin convinced many leaders of Western opinion that he was a genuine enemy of Hitler's. When he told an American publisher that "we have constructed the socialist society . . . not to shackle individual liberty, but that the human personality may feel itself really free," large segments of Western society took his words at face value. In the United States, university-bred young Communists, recruited during the depression, became active in government bureaus, research organizations, newspapers, publishing houses, the theater, the movies and trade unions. Such books and articles written during this period as described actual conditions in Russia were often labeled "red-baiting," and their authors, whether correspondents who had spent years there or Soviet citizens who had escaped to freedom, were denounced as "accomplices of Fascism." In the heyday of the popular front, it was convenient to ignore what was going on in Russia.

programs to combat the Communists, and finally rid all but a few unions of their influence. These programs laid the foundation for American labor's present worldwide battle against the Kremlin through the International Confederation of Free Trade Unions.

and citations, they tried to prove that Russian villages enjoyed "unprecedented freedom," peasant deaths of 1932-33 were not "really" from famine, Stalin was no dictator.

MILLIONAIRE Corliss Lamont, son of a J. P. Morgan partner, headed "American Friends of the Soviet Union" and hailed the Stalin regime for its "splendid accomplishments."

PROLETARIAN Harry Bridges, top man among Pacific Coast longshoremen since 1937, backed Communist causes but stated, "I neither affirm nor deny I am a Communist."

PURGED

ZINOVIEV

PURGED

KAMENEV

SUICIDE

TOMSKY

SUDDEN

ORDZHONIKIDZE

INCREDIBLE "confessions" marked the public trials of former Communist leaders. But while the eyes of western correspondents and diplomats were riveted on the prisoners' dock in Moscow, hundreds, then thousands, of other Communists and high officials of Soviet government and industry were being shot without "confessing." Trade union chief Tomsky's suicide in 1936, and Ordzhonikidze's death two weeks after his immediate subordinate Piatakov was executed, gave only a vague hint of what the Kremlin was doing behind

PURGES rock Party;

old Communist chiefs 'confess' in Moscow trials

The Soviet leaders of Lenin's day had traveled far since 1922, when Judge Piatakov condemned to death twelve defiant Socialist Revolutionaries. When Judge Ulrich opened the Moscow court on August 19, 1936, the dock was filled by sixteen former Bolshevik chiefs, headed by Lenin's comrades Zinoviev and Kamenev. Since their expulsion from the Party in 1927, their repeated declarations of loyalty to Stalin had robbed them of all authority. What was in store for them had been suggested when Sergei Kirov, Party chief in Leningrad, was assassinated by a young Communist in 1934. Kirov's death was attributed to a "White Guard" conspiracy, but Zinoviev and Kamenev had pleaded guilty to "moral complicity" in 1935 and had gone to prison. Now they were charged with belonging to a giant conspiracy, directed from abroad by exiled Leon Trotsky in collusion with Nazi Germany. According to Prosecutor Vishinsky, the accused had admitted, after months of thorough probing by Henry Yagoda's GPU, that they had plotted to kill Stalin, Ordzhonikidze and other Politburo members. Under Vishinsky's guidance, they repeated their confessions in court. Vishinsky's summation ended with the words, "I demand that dogs gone mad be shot—every one of them." All sixteen were convicted and shot; Trotsky was convicted *in absentia*. In January 1937, the same court condemned another group of leading Communists, headed by Radek and Piatakov, the judge in the Socialist Revolutionary Trial. In November, Abram Gotz, the leader of the Socialist Revolutionaries imprisoned under suspended death sentence since the 1922 trial, was executed; the other Socialist leaders were shot later. While these executions were taking place, Party propagandists sang paeans to Stalin.

RISING young Georgi Malenkov, of Stalin's own secretariat, was valuable during the purges because of his card-index mind.

"GREETINGS TO COMRADE STALIN" SAYS BIG SIGN FRONT AND CENTER

DEATH	PURGED	PURGED	PURGED

LIES IN STATE	PIATAKOV	SEREBRIAKOV	RADEK

the scenes. As for the Old Bolshevik "confessors"—men like former Comintern chief Zinoviev, former Moscow Party leader Kamenev, former Central Committee member Piatakov, former Party secretary Serebriakov, and former propaganda ace Radek— they had them-selves helped forge the Communist doctrine that the welfare of the Party was the supreme moral law. At the demand of the Party, they had been "confessing" heresies ever since Lenin's death. This final self-debasement was the product of years of moral disintegration.

MOSCOW PARADES LIKE THIS ONE IN 1936 WERE STAGED BY STALIN'S MACHINE TO CONVINCE THE WORLD THAT THE PEOPLE SUPPORTED HIS PURGES

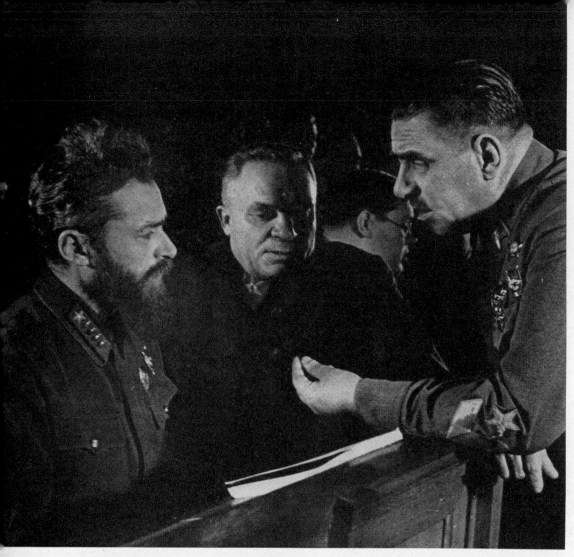

DOOMED Red Army leaders—General Gamarnik, political chief; Marshal Yegorov, Chief of Staff; Marshal Bluecher, Far East commander—confer in the Kremlin, 1936.

FANFARE marking exhibition of the giant airliner *Maxim Gorky* in 1936 brought together a group of leading Soviet generals and airmen, most of whom were shot in the great Red Army purge of 1937-38. Tupolev, the noted plane designer (cap and white shirt), was jailed but was later released. Third from the left is War Commissar Voroshilov.

SURVIVORS of Stalin's war against the Red Army included his civil war comrades Klim Voroshilov (right, with Stalin a few months before the purges) and Semyon Budyenny.

DEATH hovered over the 1937 May Day Parade in Red Square. Below, the leaders of the Red Army, Tukhachevsky, Bielov, Voroshilov, Yegorov and Budyenny. Tukhachevsky was shot six weeks later, Bielov and Yegorov not long after. Above, Stalin (left) and other Politburo members. The man in the center is Yezhov, new secret police chief.

ARMY PURGES kill off top generals, suspected of plot to overthrow Stalin

Moscow announced on May 31, 1937 that Deputy War Commissar Ian Gamarnik, director of the Political Department of the Red Army, had committed suicide. On June 12, the official press told the world that nine leading generals of the Red Army had been secretly tried, condemned to death and shot, all within 48 hours. According to the published verdict, they had "violated their military oath, betrayed their country, betrayed the peoples of the U.S.S.R., betrayed the Red Army." The top victim, Marshal Tukhachevsky, had been one of the most

brilliant commanders of the civil war and had been largely responsible for mechanizing the Red Army. Within a few months, nearly all the generals who had signed Tukhachevsky's death warrant were themselves liquidated without trial; none of them confessed. Before long, almost all the eighty members of the Soviet War Council (as it was set up in 1934) were shot or had disappeared. The purge eliminated the Navy and Air Force command as well—an estimated total of 30,000 officers. The Kremlin has never published any documentary evidence to

support its charge that the generals had plotted with Nazi Germany; nor in the mass of Gestapo, Nazi Party and German High Command documents captured by the Allies in 1945 was a single scrap of paper found linking the executed generals (or Trotsky or the Old Bolsheviks) with a Nazi plot; nor did the Soviet prosecutor at the war crimes trials attempt to cross-examine Nazi leaders on the subject. Whether these generals had indeed plotted to overthrow Stalin and build a more normal regime in Russia, remains one of the Kremlin's abundant mysteries.

BUKHARIN

RYKOV

CHAINED by Party loyalty, but disillusioned by what Communism had brought to Russia, Bukharin told the court: "While I was in prison, I made a re-evaluation of my entire past. For when you ask yourself, 'If you must die, what are you dying for?', an absolute black vacuity

rises before you with startling vividness." Lenin's sister Maria is shown with him in the *Pravda* office. Ex-Premier Rykov, above with Voroshilov and Stalin, had often tried to stem the terror. The most humane Communist leader, Rykov died a completely broken man.

MORE PURGES destroy

ex-Premier, 'Pravda' editor, two GPU chiefs

The remnants of Lenin's Old Guard were tried in March 1938. This time the main actors were former Premier Alexei Rykov and Nicholas Bukharin, whom Lenin had described as "not only the most valuable theoretician of the Party, as he is the biggest, but also . . . the favorite of the entire Party." Rykov and Bukharin had dropped from the Party high command in 1929, but Stalin had retained their services—Bukharin had drafted the Soviet Constitution of 1936. The other defendants included former Party secretary Krestinsky, ex-GPU chief Yagoda and two Kremlin doctors. Again Trotsky was named as the main instigator of all the alleged crimes. The state charged that Rykov and Bukharin had been traitors since the first days of Soviet rule; had been plotting for twenty years with the German, Polish, Japanese and British intelligence services; had tried to kill Lenin in 1918; had, with Yagoda and the Kremlin physicians, poisoned various deceased Soviet leaders as well as the novelist Maxim Gorky. In the courtroom, Krestinsky repudiated his prison confession, but capitulated after a recess; others "confessed" on a grand scale. Bukharin, however, managed to tell the court that "in the period of the liquidation of the kulaks, in 1929-30, we pitied the expropriated kulaks from so-called humanitarian motives" and that during industrialization he had regarded "with anger at bottom, our huge, gigantically growing factories as monstrous gluttons which consumed everything, deprived the broad masses of articles of consumption." Yet, in his final statement, he also paid homage to Stalin and the Party. The Moscow trials were investigated by an international commission headed by Professor John Dewey, with John F. Finerty, former counsel for Sacco and Vanzetti, as counsel. Its two-volume report ended, "The confessions themselves contain such inherent improbabilities as to convince the commission that they do not represent the truth, irrespective of any means used to obtain them." After the execution of Rykov and Bukharin, Party textbooks were rewritten to brand all members of Lenin's Politburo, except Stalin, as lifelong traitors and agents of foreign powers. Stalin edited one of the new books.

CONDEMNED *in absentia* by the Moscow court, Trotsky was forced out of Norway by Soviet pressure in 1936. Above, in Coyoacan, Mexico he began dictating his long biography of Stalin. "Stalin's first qual fication," he wrote, "was a contemptuous attitude toward ideas.

PURGER PURGED

PURGED

POISONED?

PURGES PURGER

YAGODA

YENUKIDZE

GORKY

YEZHOV

CARNAGE of 1937-38 under Nicholas Yezhov, Yagoda's successor as GPU head, killed thousands of engineers, factory directors and ordinary citizens, and nearly all the "Old Bolsheviks," including Stalin's closest friends of Georgian days, such as Abel Yenukidze (above) and Budu Mdivani. Correspondents counted reports of more than 5000 executions in the official Soviet press. Several hundred thousand more victims went to labor camps. Then Stalin purged Yezhov and replaced him with a fellow-Georgian, Lavrenti Beria.

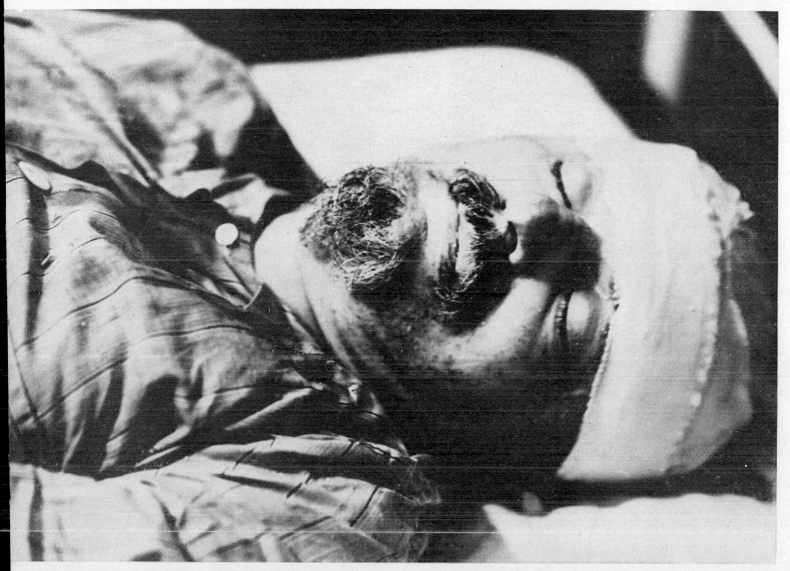

PICKAXE blow to the brain on August 20, 1940 finished Trotsky's work. A few months earlier, a group of twenty-five to thirty men in Mexican police uniforms had fired 300 machine gun bullets through his bedroom window. The successful executioner, known as "Frank Jacson" and "Jacques Mornard," blurted out immediately after being seized and disarmed. "They made me do it! They made me do it! They have imprisoned my mother!" Then he refused to say more. Sentenced to twenty years in prison, he has remained silent to this day.

MOSCOW ART THEATER on its fortieth anniversary, October 17, 1938, posed with Stalin and his Politburo. Founded by Stanislavsky and Nemirovich-Danchenko (bearded, next to Stalin), its greatest actors were Moskvin (bow tie, between Voroshilov and Molotov) and Kach-

alov (seated, second from right). In its early days and even under Lenin, the theater produced dramas of social protest and new experimental forms, but Stalin barred them. The little man in uniform standing behind Molotov is secret police chief Yezhov, soon to vanish.

DEFIANT Vsevolod Meyerhold, actor (as above) and theatrical director, told a public meeting in June 1939, "In your effort to eradicate 'formalism,' you have destroyed art." Next day he disappeared. His wife was murdered soon afterwards.

SYCOPHANT writer Alexei Tolstoy, a man of considerable literary talent, gained Stalin's favor and huge royalties with propaganda novels which justified the dictatorship by twisted historical comparisons. He admitted he wrote for money.

HOUNDED film director Eisenstein (*Potemkin, Ten Days That Shook the World*) "confessed" in 1946 that "the sense of historical truth betrayed me in ... part of *Ivan the Terrible*." The movie, Eisenstein's last, was a veiled attack on dictatorship.

BROWBEATEN Shostakovich said he would "reform," after his music displeased Stalin in 1936. But in 1948 the Party attacked him again. He admitted that he had "swerved to the side of formalism" and promised to write simpler melodies in the future.

ARTISTS struggle to safeguard
Russian culture against Stalin's bigoted taste

The Soviet intellectual purge did not halt with rewriting history; Stalin waged war on all non-conventional literature, painting and music. Artists who bowed to his bigoted taste received lavish rewards, as long as they composed odes and cantatas presenting him as the heir of Russia's tradition. Non-conformists, whether philosophers, poets, historians, critics, theatrical directors or humorists, either were exiled or they simply disappeared. Party theories of art were shaped by Stalin's reactions; a work hailed as a masterpiece one day was often condemned at Stalin's frown the next. While the Kremlin's tame artists lived in fear-ridden splendor, tougher minds protected their integrity and their lives by translating foreign works and editing Russian classics. To escape the blight, millions of Russians turned to Pushkin, Tolstoy and other great writers whose works had not been banned.

HARDLY CHANGED BY DECADES OF SOVIET RULE, THE RUSSIAN BALLET

TRAGIC FATE of the Moscow Art Theater was reflected in its being forced to produce more and more Communist plays such as *Land* (above), which depicted as "kulaks" and "enemies of the people" the rebellious Tambov peasants who had resisted Cheka grain requi-

sitioning squads in the early years of Communist rule. Despite the rigid controls, directors and actors of the Moscow Art Theater and other Soviet theaters are still criticized by Communist spokesmen for portraying "White Guard" and foreign villains too sympathetically.

REMAINS THE SAME AS IN THE DAYS WHEN PAVLOVA DANCED—ABOVE, A PERFORMANCE OF ACT FOUR OF TCHAIKOVSKY'S 'SWAN LAKE' IN MOSCOW

WOMEN of Riga, the capital of Latvia, tearfully receive the news that their government was granting naval and air bases on the Baltic to the Soviet Union, under the pistol-point Soviet-Latvian treaty of October 5, 1939. The following June, the Soviets demanded that puppet governments be established in Estonia and Lithuania as well as Latvia. Communist-supervised elections were conducted, and on July 21, the three Communist-controlled parliaments voted to ask for admission into the Soviet Union. Their "request" was granted.

DEFENDERS of tiny Estonia gathered around a World War I tank in the market place of Narva, near the Soviet border, and prepared to fight the Red Army. The Estonian government, knowing that such resistance would mean suicide, bowed to Stalin on September 28, 1939.

RED FLEET admiral, commanding the warship *October Revolution*, went ashore at Tallin, the capital of Estonia, to set up a Soviet naval base under the "mutual aid" pact. Soviet force put an end to the independence which the Baltic states had enjoyed for two decades.

PRISONERS captured by the Finns in January 1940 were inadequately clothed for winter warfare. In the last month of the war, the Red Army moved superbly equipped elite troops, motorized sledges and ski detachments into the line against dwindling Finnish manpower.

THREATENED by Stalin,
Baltic states surrender, but Finns fight back

With Poland partitioned, Stalin began to move into the Baltic states, as agreed by the Ribbentrop-Molotov protocol. Threatened by military attack, Estonia signed a "mutual assistance" pact ceding naval and air bases. Lithuania and Latvia were forced to follow suit. These concessions did not satisfy Stalin. A year later, the Baltic states were forcibly incorporated into the Soviet Union. Finland rejected similar demands, and on November 29, 1939, the Red Army invaded the country. Expecting a quick victory, Moscow announced the creation on the Soviet-Finnish frontier of a "people's government" headed by Comintern veteran Otto Kuusinen. But Russian troops showed little enthusiasm for the war. For three months, the Finnish Army, which never had more than 120,000 men on the crucial Karelian isthmus front, held off the Red Army until massed Soviet artillery finally cracked the Mannerheim line. In all, Stalin needed 47 divisions, one army corps of light and medium tanks, two brigades of heavy tanks and over 3000 planes to force the Finnish government to conclude peace, on March 12. The Finns lost the Karelian isthmus and Hangoe naval base, but remained free.

CASUALTIES from hunger and cold were heavy when Russian supply lines were cut in 22-below-zero weather during Kemi River battle. Letters from home found on the dead stressed the war's unpopularity; survivors had to abandon equipment like the Stalin portrait above.

PUPPET Finnish regime under Communist Kuusinen (extreme right) was quickly set up by Stalin after the Soviet invasion. Here Molotov signs a treaty with the new "government"; Zhdanov, Voroshilov and Stalin watch. Kuusinen's regime was shelved when Finland resisted.

POILUS LIKE THIS SENTRY ON THE MAGINOT LINE PAID HEAVILY FOR THEIR LEADERS' BELIEF THAT STATIC DEFENSE COULD CONTAIN HITLER

WESTERN FRONT crumbles before the full power of Germany's armies

The false calm on the western front ended on May 10, 1940, when the Nazi army and air force attacked neutral Holland and Belgium and struck France. In 1914, the Germans had had to split their forces to meet a Russian offensive on the eastern front. In 1940, the Nazi-Soviet pact relieved them of this necessity. Such was Hitler's confidence in Stalin that, according to his Chief of Staff, he left "no more than a light covering force, scarcely fit for collecting customs duties" to face Russia. France was overwhelmed by 126 divisions, an armored juggernaut including 1000 heavy tanks, and swarms of new fighters and dive-bombers. On June 10, Mussolini stabbed her from the rear. On the 14th, Paris fell. On the 18th, Molotov summoned the German Ambassador and "expressed the warmest congratulations of the Soviet government on the splendid success of the German armed forces." On the 22nd, Marshal Petain capitulated. The Germans occupied Northern France, including Paris, but permitted Petain and Laval to set up a rump state in the south. The French Communist Party, which had called the Nazi-Soviet pact a "factor making for peace" and had spread defeatism in the French army before and during the German attack, now denounced General de Gaulle, leader of the Free French, and issued a circular declaring that "French imperialism has just sustained the greatest defeat in its history. . . . The working class, not only in France, but the world over, should regard this development as a victory for its interests, because it means one enemy less. . . . To put it briefly, the interests of the French people coincide with those of German imperialism in the latter's struggle against French imperialism and it is not . . . too much to say that for the moment German imperialism is the French people's ally. The man who does not grasp this is no revolutionary."

SMASHED by Nazi armor and air power, neutral Belgium was occupied in May 1940. Denmark and Norway, also neutral, had been overrun a month before. Above, the debris of a Belgian cyclist section, scattered by the strafing of Goering's Stukas.

FORCED by unemployment to work in German factories and mines, hundreds of thousands of French workers (like the Parisian at the left) joined the 1,500,000 French war prisoners in Germany. Some were not returned to France for years.

THE COMMUNISTS AND PRO-FASCISTS FED HIM DEFEATIST PROPAGANDA

KING **CHRISTIAN** of Denmark (shown on the first anniversary of Nazi occupation) prevented excesses by threatening to abdicate. In October 1942, Berlin demanded that Denmark impose anti-Jewish laws; the King replied by attending services in a Copenhagen synagogue.

LAVAL was France's Vice-Premier when Marshal Pétain concluded a separate peace with Hitler. He worked closely with the Nazis, helped introduce racial laws and concentration camps in unoccupied French territory, and conscripted French labor for German war industry.

89

COMMUNISTS in America opposed lend-lease aid to Britain, demanding that "no further aid be given British imperialism." Union locals under their domination went on strike and tied up Vultee Aircraft, North American Aircraft, Allis-Chalmers and other defense plants.

BRITAIN fights for her life while Communists denounce 'warmonger Churchill'

When France fell, Hitler was convinced that Britain would have to sue for an early peace. The British army had left its armor on the beaches of Dunkirk. Home defenses amounted to little more than 1000 trained RAF pilots, some barbed wire and a few road blocks. "The whole fury and might of the enemy must very soon be turned on us," Winston Churchill told Britain on June 18, 1940. "Hitler knows that he will have to break us on this island or lose the war. If we can stand up to him, all Europe may be free.... Let us therefore brace ourselves to our duties and so bear ourselves that, if the British Empire and its Commonwealth last for a thousand years, men will say, 'This was their finest hour.'" Eleven days later, Hitler began launching mass air assaults against the cities of Britain, and his general staff prepared invasion plans. From the Soviet Union, meanwhile, Stalin continued to ship him grain, oil and other strategic materials, despite the British ambassador's warning that Germany was "striving for the hegemony of Europe." Communist spokesmen all over the world denounced the "warmonger Churchill" and the "imperialist war." In the United States, Communists helped tie up key defense plants, cooperated with the "America First" group which urged neutrality, and fought Selective Service and aid to Britain with the slogan "The Yanks Are Not Coming." On the English beaches, infantrymen with rifles and tommy guns awaited Hitler's armored legions; and overhead, a handful of young pilots pitted their skill and courage against Marshal Goering's air armada. When the RAF forced him to discontinue daylight raids, he sent his bombers over London for 57 consecutive nights. The incendiary raid of December 29, 1940, started 1500 fires, and the whole air blitz of 1940-41, "The Battle of Britain," killed 42,000 civilians. But the obstinate courage and democratic spirit of the British people as they stood alone proved stronger than Hitler's rain of fire and steel.

LONDON was bombed mercilessly in 1940-41 and then again in 1944, when the population was blasted with "buzz-bombs" and huge rockets.

SHORE DEFENSE of England in 1940 rested with 20,000 trained troops, 200 guns, 50 tanks. Above, a battery on the southeastern coast.

MOLOTOV, arriving in Berlin on November 12, 1940 to confer with Nazi leaders, was given a salute and honor guard. Stalin sent him in response to Hitler's invitation.

GOERING could not stifle the RAF, so one of its raids interrupted Molotov's visit.

WORRIED by Britain's dogged stand, Berlin, Moscow and Tokyo plot next moves

As the war with Britain continued, Nazi industry could no longer meet Germany's armament needs without cutting shipments of material promised to the U.S.S.R. by the Nazi-Soviet trade agreement of February 1940. On the other hand, such a cut might provoke Stalin to retaliate by suspending his deliveries of grain and oil. A German official noted that Russia had yielded almost a million tons of grain, as well as "petroleum, cotton, precious and nonferrous metals, phosphates," and these, he emphasized, had been "a very substantial prop to the German war economy." Meanwhile, additional tension developed over the movement of German troops through Finland, and over the Berlin-Rome-Tokyo alliance of September 27, 1940, despite

Ribbentrop's assurance that it was "directed exclusively against American warmongers." To heal the breach, Stalin sent Molotov to Berlin in November. Hitler assured him that "Germany was not seeking to obtain military aid from Russia" but that there were "certain sources of raw materials which were considered by Germany as most vital and absolutely indispensable." Molotov then asked about the Soviet place in the new Tripartite Pact, and about Soviet interests in Bulgaria, Rumania and Turkey, as well as in Finland. Hitler's answers were evasive. A month later, Hitler issued a secret directive to his armed forces to prepare to "crush Soviet Russia in a quick campaign [Operation Barbarossa] even before the conclusion of the war against England."

RIBBENTROP (extreme left) told Japanese Foreign Minister Matsuoka on March 27, 1941 that "Germany was certain that a campaign against Russia would end in the absolute victory of German arms and the total crushing of the Russian Army and Russian State," and that the German-Italian-Japanese pact had "above all the goal of frightening America into abandoning the course it had chosen and of keeping it out of the war." Matsuoka mentioned that some Japanese felt that a conflict with the U. S. "would involve a five- or ten-year war."

HESS was Hitler's second deputy until he flew to Scotland with "peace" bid in 1941.

HITLER did not settle economic and territorial issues with Molotov on November 13.

At Hitler's right: Ribbentrop and General Keitel, later executed as war criminals.

STALIN wished Matsuoka (left) a good journey at the Moscow railroad station after they had concluded the Soviet-Japanese non-aggression pact of April 13, 1941. Matsuoka informed Italy's envoy to Moscow that Stalin had told him he was "a convinced adherent of the Axis and an opponent of England and America." Matsuoka assured the German ambassador that the new treaty "in no way affects the Three-Power Pact." Talking with the Japanese, Stalin was unusually animated. "We are both Asiatics," the Georgian declared.

TOWNS LIKE THESE FELL QUICKLY TO HITLER'S INVADING PANZERS AND INFANTRY DIVISIONS IN THE EARLY MONTHS OF THE RUSSIAN CAMPAIGN

HITLER veers east, hurls undefeated Wehrmacht against Russia in supreme gamble

Hitler's plans became clear when his troops massed in Poland and East Prussia. Stalin moved Red Army forces westward, but renewed his attempts to placate Hitler. The German foreign office noted that during March 1941, Soviet shipments to Germany "rose by leaps and bounds." In April, Stalin threw his arms around German Ambassador Schulenburg and said, "We must remain friends, and you must do everything to that end." Russia delivered 208,000 tons of grain and 90,000 tons of petroleum that month. In May, Stalin succeeded Molotov as Premier, recognized the pro-Nazi Iraq regime, and closed the Belgian, Norwegian and Yugoslav embassies in Moscow, but continued to match Hitler's divisions on the frontier. "At no time in Russian history," said the Soviet Minister to Sweden, "have there been stronger troop contingents assembled on Russia's western borders than now." At 9:30 P.M., June 21, Molotov asked Schulenburg what had caused "the present situation." A few hours later, Nazi planes were bombing Zhitomir, Kiev and Sevastopol.

CHURCHILL pledged "we shall give whatever help we can to Russia and the Russian people" on the day that Hitler invaded the country. Above, on July 30, Churchill, Polish Premier Sikorski, Eden and Soviet envoy Maisky sign a nullification of the Nazi-Soviet pact.

ATLANTIC CHARTER, issued by Roosevelt and Churchill at their shipboard meeting off Newfoundland in August 1941, voiced their hopes for a peace which would "afford assurance that all the men in all the lands may live out their lives in freedom from fear and want."

MOSCOW heard loudspeakers announce on June 22, 1941, "At four o'clock this morning . . . without a declaration of war, German troops assaulted our country. . . . This is not the first time our people have had to deal with an arrogant invading enemy. At the time of Napo-

leon's campaign in Russia, our people replied with a patriotic war, and Napoleon was defeated and met his end. Arrogant Hitler, who has launched a new campaign against our country, will suffer the same fate." This Moscow photo was taken as the news of war was broadcast.

ENDLESS COLUMNS OF SOVIET PRISONERS, LIKE THESE TAKEN EAST OF KIEV IN SEPTEMBER 1941, LED HITLER TO THINK RUSSIA WAS DEFEATED

CHEERS for the advancing Wehrmacht, somewhere on the Soviet-German front, expressed the premature joy of the peasants. Believing they would be allowed to till their own soil, peasants in White Russia and the Ukraine dissolved collective farms as soon as the Communist authorities left. But German military government was instructed to retain the collectives, in order to expedite grain shipments to the Reich. The Nazis soon aroused fierce hatred through what one German official called their "limitless abuse of Slavic humanity."

ON THIS SECTOR ALONE, THE GERMANS TOOK 665,000 PRISONERS. MORE THAN 3,000,000 RED TROOPS SURRENDERED IN THE FIRST EIGHT MONTHS

WELCOME startles Germans, alarms Stalin

Hitler hurled against Russia 121 divisions and over 2700 planes. The Red Army met them with 119 of its 155 divisions, supported by 5000 planes. Unlike the Russian Army of World War I, the Soviet Army was as well equipped in modern weapons as was its foe. Still, the Germans advanced rapidly across Russia, taking more than 2,000,000 prisoners in the first four months. On some sectors, notably around Smolensk, the Russians resisted furiously; but in the main, they showed less fight than any troops in Russian history. Their mass surrenders and the friendly welcome of many villages surprised the Wehrmacht. It did not surprise Stalin. On July 31, 1941, he told President Roosevelt's personal envoy, Harry Hopkins, that the peoples under the Nazi yoke and "countless other millions still unconquered could receive the kind of encouragement and moral strength they needed to resist Hitler from only one source, and that was the United States." He asked Hopkins to report that he would "welcome American troops on any part of the Russian front under the complete command of the American army." On September 15, with the German Army approaching Moscow and Leningrad, he wired Churchill, "It seems to me that Great Britain could without risk land in Archangel twenty-five to thirty divisions or transport them across Iran to the southern regions of the U.S.S.R." Stalin had many more divisions than the United States and Britain combined, but little reason to be confident that they would fight to preserve his regime. He therefore appealed to traditional patriotism and told Russia that its battle was part of "the struggle of the peoples of Europe and America for their independence and democratic freedoms."

GENERAL ANDREI VLASOV fought under Marshal Zhukov in the defense of Moscow. When captured by the Germans, he formed an anti-Stalin corps, but Hitler would not permit him to recruit a full-fledged Russian liberation army. In 1945, he surrendered to the U. S. army in Czechoslovakia, was turned over to the Soviets and hanged in Moscow.

BOUQUETS greeted the German soldiers above when they entered this village in the Ukraine. Collectivization-made famine had deepened the population's hatred of Communist rule, but Nazi brutality soon turned the people against the Germans, and partisan warfare began.

RED ARMY men like these Volga Tartars enlisted in the Wehrmacht. "We raised 45,000 Cossacks," a German officer reported. "Some of these were genuine Cossacks. . . . Others were Russians who posed as Cossacks." All told, half a million Soviet soldiers fought Stalin.

NAZIS hanged, then photographed, these Russian civilians in the summer of 1941, near Smolensk. Moscow gave wide publicity to such pictures, as evidence that the Nazis were not fighting Communism, but were waging a war of extermination against the Russian people.

SS CHIEF HEINRICH HIMMLER, DIRECTOR OF MASS MURDERS IN POLAND AND RUSSIA, VISITED UKRAINIAN PEASANT VILLAGES IN AUGUST 1941

CONTEMPT and brutality of Nazis toward Russians awakens their patriotism

Hitler, who had said that he was making war on "the Bolshevist center in Moscow," chose instead to make war on the Russian people. The German army, as a matter of official policy, did not feed Russian civilians or prisoners of war. A top secret German document in February 1942 revealed that of 3,600,000 Soviet prisoners of war, "only several hundred thousand are still able to work fully. A large part has starved or died. . . . In the majority of cases, the camp commanders have forbidden the civilian population to put food at the disposal of prisoners." This policy fired the patriotism of the Red Army and of the civilian population.

A German official warned that if Hitler's policy did not change, "the power of resistance of the Red Army and the whole Russian people will mount still more, and Germany must continue to sacrifice her best blood." But it was too late. As Stalin remarked, "They are not fighting for the system, they are fighting for their soil."

FLOGGING by the Nazis did not cow Russia's farmers; instead, it enabled Stalin to rally the people behind him as the lesser evil.

MASS MURDER awaited these Jewish civilians herded into ravines and tank traps. In 1941 the Nazis killed some 52,000 in Kiev alone.

RUSSIAN PRISONERS were moved in open freight cars in subzero cold. A German report complained that "there is no sense transporting manpower in open and unheated cars because . . . we have only corpses to unload." In the last four months of 1941, 500,000 died.

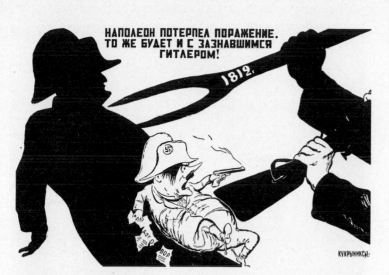

НАПОЛЕОН ПОТЕРПЕЛ ПОРАЖЕНИЕ.
ТО ЖЕ БУДЕТ И С ЗАЗНАВШИМСЯ
ГИТЛЕРОМ!

1812.

КУКРЫНИКСЫ

PATRIOTISM was evoked by giant posters reminding the Russian people that "Napoleon suffered defeat; so will arrogant Hitler." Against the heroic shadow of Napoleon in 1812, Hitler—a torn-up treaty in one hand and a pistol in the other—makes an absurd figure.

LENINGRAD defenses held firm, although the city was surrounded and many of its inhabitants starved. Above, anti-aircraft guns, 1942.

DEFIANT Russian armies hold off
Germans at Leningrad, hit back from Moscow

With the Wehrmacht twenty miles from Moscow, the Red Army fought bitterly for Russia's survival. From Lenin's mausoleum in Red Square Stalin told front-bound Russian troops on November 6, 1941, "May the manly images of our great ancestors—Alexander Nevsky, Dmitri Donskoy, Kuzma Minin, Dmitri Pozharsky, Alexander Suvorov and Mikhail Kutuzov—inspire you in this war!" Not even his sudden evocation of Russia's past heroes, whom Communists had long reviled, could quell the panic that now gripped officials in the city. Following the evacuation of government offices to Kuibyshev on the Volga (Stalin himself remained in the Kremlin), Party members tore up their cards, while the people of Moscow prepared to settle accounts with them. Outside the city, the Russian armies under Marshal Zhukov took the offensive and drove back the Wehrmacht. On December 8, Hitler announced that he was suspending operations for the winter. His blitzkrieg had failed and his "crusade against Bolshevism" had turned, as a result of his war against the Russian people, into a bloodletting contest between two great nations, to be settled in gigantic battles on a thousand-mile front. As long as that fierce struggle raged, the Russian armies and people had one enemy: the Wehrmacht. As long as German troops were on Russian soil, the Russians had one aim: to drive them out.

TRENCHES were dug in Leningrad (above) and Moscow all through the stern winter of 1941-42 to halt the Nazis' onrushing panzer units.

PARTISANS took to the woods, leaving their farms behind, to blow up bridges and ammunition dumps, harass German communication lines.

AIR RAID shelter in the western Krasnaya Presnia district, Moscow, also had a patriotic poster. Woman in beret is the air raid warden.

TRUCK convoys carried U. S. supplies from the Persian Gulf over this highway to Russia. To speed delivery, U. S. built two inlet ports.

"SONG of Struggle and Friendship" was the title of this closing tableau on Moscow stage during the Anglo-Russian-American alliance.

ALLIES rush planes, trucks, food and guns to help Russia roll back the Wehrmacht

Courage had saved Russia, but the price had been tremendous, not only in lives but in resources. In less than five months, the German armies had occupied territory which produced 65 per cent of Russia's coal, 58 per cent of her steel, 60 per cent of her aluminum and 38 per cent of her grain. Behind the Urals, factories worked around the clock but could not meet her army's needs. Britain sent her as much as could be spared—more than 2400 tanks and 1800 planes by mid-1942; a voluntary British "Aid to Russia" organization, headed by Mrs. Winston Churchill, sent medical and surgical supplies. But by far the greatest support came from the United States. A few weeks after Germany attacked, American shipping and supply agencies arranged to send Russia $9,000,000 worth of materials. In November 1941, President Roosevelt declared her eligible for lend-lease. Between October 1, 1941 and May 31, 1945, 2660 ships sailed from American ports with 16,529,791 tons of supplies for Russia. Of this total, 15,234,791 tons arrived; fifty-two ships were diverted to meet urgent British needs, and seventy-two were sunk by Nazi U-boats and planes. In the worst period, March-July 1942, twenty-seven U. S. ships were lost on the Murmansk run. British losses were equally heavy. After one British convoy had battled through, the Soviet Army newspaper, *Red Star*, cried, "The Germans have shattered themselves against the undaunted spirit of the English. Glory to the English sailors! They are bringing tanks, bombs, shells, and grain to those fighting for freedom."

Such tributes were rare, however, and as the Nazi danger abated, the Kremlin played down American and British aid. The supplies continued to flow notwithstanding. By mid-1943, the U. S. had sent 4100 planes, 138,000 trucks and jeeps, 912,000 tons of steel; American contributions to Russian War Relief supplemented military aid with medical supplies, bandages and clothing. Through May 1945, America sent 4,478,116 tons of food, 2,670,371 tons of petroleum products, and 1900 steam locomotives. The United States also sent machinery and industrial equipment, aircraft spare parts, surface vehicles and weapons, as well as vast quantities of clothing and boots for the Red Army. Despite Stalin's reluctance to publicize American lend-lease, Russian troops knew they were eating American food, wearing American-made uniforms and rolling forward in American vehicles. Americans in Russia reported that the moral effect was tremendous. The Russian Army sang American songs; "Willys" became Russian for jeep and "Studebaker" the Russian GI's slang for anything superlative, including his favorite girl. To millions of Russians, deprived for a generation of their liberty, President Roosevelt, with whom they identified American aid, became the symbol of their hopes for a freer future. In the words of one American diplomat, "What impressed the Russians most deeply was that in a hard world in which authority was not normally benevolent, here was a powerful leader who had extended the hand of friendship . . . in an hour of need."

NORTH ATLANTIC CONVOYS FOUGHT THEIR WAY THROUGH U-BOAT INFESTED WATERS, PAST NAZI FIGHTER BASES AND SUBMARINE PENS IN NORWAY

AMERICA entered the war when the Japanese attacked Pearl Harbor on December 7, 1941. Already "the arsenal of democracy," the U. S. now mobilized 11,600,000 men and sent its soldiers, sailors and airmen to battle stations in Europe, Africa, Asia and the Western Pacific.

TO DELIVER LEND-LEASE PLANES, TANKS AND GUNS AT THE ARCTIC PORTS OF ARCHANGEL AND MURMANSK FOR THE EMBATTLED RUSSIAN ARMIES

AFTER THEIR SMASHING VICTORY AT STALINGRAD, RUSSIAN SOLDIERS LIKE THESE TOOK THE OFFENSIVE AND DROVE THE NAZIS TO THE DNIEPER

COUNTERATTACK drives Nazis from Stalingrad and North Africa; Allies

In 1943, the Allies moved to the offensive throughout the world. On malaria-infested islands in the Southwest Pacific, American, Australian and British forces were driving back through Japanese pillboxes, swamps and jungles. In Germany, the all-out air war which Hitler had started with his saturation-bombing of Guernica in 1937, now rebounded in full fury; in March, the RAF dropped 900 tons of bombs in each of its first two major raids on Berlin. In Russia, the Red Army forged a steel ring around the twenty-two Nazi divisions at Stalingrad, then stormed 500 miles northwest to defeat the Wehrmacht in a gigantic tank battle at Kursk in July; by October, it stood on the banks of the Dnieper, across from Kiev. In North Africa, American and British forces opened a new front; the British Eighth Army defeated Rommel in Libya, and by May all Axis forces had been driven out of Tunisia; 250,000 German and Italian prisoners remained behind. In July, the western Allies landed in Sicily; in September, on the Italian mainland. And throughout the whole year, Nazi-Fascist troops in the occupied territories were harried by

TEARS of joy greeted this Russian officer liberating Bryansk after thirteen months of German occupation. When the Red Army reentered the city, it found little more than a charred shell; such citizens as survived had done so by hiding for months in nearby forests.

BASS VIOLIN was saved by its bombed-out owner during the battle of Stalingrad. The German disaster here, writes Churchill, ended Hitler's "prodigious effort to conquer Russia by force of arms and destroy Communism by an equally odious form of totalitarian tyranny."

THESE GERMANS PREFERRED SURRENDER TO DYING FOR ADOLF HITLER

NAZI SS OFFICER IN WARSAW REMOVING BEARD OF AN ORTHODOX JEW

'ROUTED FROM BUNKERS BY FORCE' SAID THE NAZI PICTURE CAPTION

land in Italy; the Japanese start falling back

Soviet guerillas, French maquis, Serbian chetniks and Croat partisans. Meanwhile, Propaganda Minister Joseph Goebbels complained in his diary for that March that the deportation of the last Jewish residents of Berlin was sabotaged "because unfortunately, our better circles, especially the intellectuals, once again have failed to understand our policy about the Jews and in some cases have even taken their part. As a result our plans were tipped off prematurely, so that a lot of Jews slipped through our hands. But we will catch them yet." And he caught them.

THESE JEWISH 'PRISONERS' WERE KILLED AFTER THE GHETTO BATTLE

HITLER'S WAR ON THE JEWS

In the midst of World War II, the Nazis deported more than five million Jewish men, women and children from all parts of Europe, first to ghettos, then to extermination camps in Maidanek, Auschwitz and elsewhere in occupied Poland. Here they were gassed to death and incinerated. Most of the Warsaw Ghetto had been exterminated by starvation; the rest died in a battle against SS troops in April 1943; the SS chief reported 56,065 killed in this single operation. In occupied Soviet areas, the Nazis murdered the Jews on the spot.

SWORD of Stalingrad, a gift from King George VI, was presented to Stalin by Churchill at the Teheran conference (November 1943) as a tribute to the heroic people of the city. Anthony Eden is at far left. Molotov is at the right of Stalin, who is kissing the red scabbard.

AMERICAN TROOPS WHO STORMED OMAHA BEACH ON D-DAY, JUNE 6, 1944, ENCOUNTERED DESPERATE GERMAN RESISTANCE IN THEIR NORMANDY DRIVE

FREE FRENCH spearhead

drive on Paris; Germans attempt to kill Hitler

Four years of totalitarian dictatorship ended in France in 1944 when Allied armies, supported by the underground French Forces of the Interior (FFI), drove out the Wehrmacht. The push required the combined power of one French, one Polish, three Canadian, fourteen British and twenty American divisions, plus an air umbrella of over 10,000 bombers and fighters, and partisan and paratroop operations behind the German lines. Allied infantry battled for every inch of ground among the hedgerows and pillboxes of Normandy, while Allied artillery and aircraft blasted rail centers and Nazi fortifications elsewhere in France. On July 20, 1944, a small group of German generals and civilians tried to end the war by killing Hitler, but he escaped with minor wounds, and their revolt was crushed. German soldiers continued to fight with tenacious courage, although a large part of the Wehrmacht had been destroyed in Russia, the Luftwaffe had been knocked from the sky, their cities were being pulverized by block-busting air raids, and Russian troops were approaching German territory from the east. In December, they still mustered enough power for a desperate counter-thrust through the Ardennes forest (The Battle of the Bulge) before they were forced to fall back to the Siegfried line. This, their last offensive, cost the Germans more than 90,000 casualties.

GIs ADVANCING THROUGH LE MANS, FRANCE, RECEIVED WARM WELCOME

PARIS rose against the Wehrmacht on August 19, 1944, a few days before the entry of Free French troops under General LeClerc. The Parisians fought from windows, rooftops, doorways and barricades with weapons which they had captured or had received by parachute.

106

BEFORE THIS FRENCH SOLDIER LANDED AGAIN ON HIS NATIVE SOIL, HIS DIVISION HAD MARCHED 1200 MILES ACROSS THE AFRICAN DESERT

OTTO ABETZ, Hitler's envoy to Paris, was sentenced in 1949 to twenty years' hard labor for crimes including deportation of French workers and theft of art treasures.

CORINNE LUCHAIRE, French film star, was sentenced in 1946 to ten years' "national indignity" for "sentimental collaboration" with the Nazis. She died four years later.

PIERRE LAVAL was sentenced to death for treason against France, for deportation of workers, and for setting up a Nazi-style police force. He was shot in October 1945.

AMERICANS liberate prisoners of war and

FDR was worn out by strains of war when he met with Stalin in February 1945 at Yalta.

Liberation came to millions as the armies of General Eisenhower and Marshal Zhukov finally cracked Hitler's home defenses and joined forces at the Elbe River on April 25, 1945. In the last weeks of the war, these armies broke into Sachsenhausen, Buchenwald, Dachau and other charnel houses, and liberated French,

Polish, Russian, British, Canadian, American, Yugoslav, Dutch, Belgian and Norwegian war prisoners, as well as millions of foreign civilians who had been pressed into work for German war industry. Some 800,000 liberated workers and prisoners trekked westward from Russian-occupied territories; millions

RUSSIAN SOLDIERS, freed by American troops from Nazi Stalag 326-6K, rushed to greet their liberators. When the European war ended, there were 750,000 Russian prisoners in Germany. The Yalta agreement required the Western Powers to send them back to the Soviet Union, but before long it became clear that the Kremlin regarded these repatriates as "traitors" and was transporting them to its own forced labor camps. Thousands of Russians in Western DP camps refused to return; some, posing as Yugoslavs

millions of enslaved workers

more moved eastward. Among those liberated by General Eisenhower's armies were some 2,000,000 Soviet citizens. From April to July, over a million of them started for home, hoping that after Russia's wartime sacrifices, the Kremlin would now behave more humanely. Others, less optimistic, preferred the DP camps.

RUSSIAN GIRLS, liberated by American troops from forced labor in a German factory, gave an ecstatic welcome to Lt. J. B. Keeley of Houston, Texas. During the spring of 1945, scenes like this were taking place throughout Germany. GI's shared their K-rations with newly released workers from all nations while the last battles were in progress.

or Poles, obtained false identity papers; others committed suicide. In February 1946, a resolution of the United Nations General Assembly stopped compulsory repatriation.

COMRADESHIP marked the Elbe River meeting of American and Russian soldiers like these at Torgau. The language barrier did not prevent understanding. Americans were as surprised to hear Russian GI's singing *K-K-K-Katie* as Russians were to hear the GI version of *Meadowland*. The marksman is Pfc. Orie Dekker of Passaic, N. J.

MUSCOVITES HELD THEIR FIRST SPONTANEOUS RALLY IN DECADES ON V-E DAY AND TOSSED AMERICAN AND BRITISH (AS HERE) SOLDIERS IN AIR

EUROPEANS and Americans rejoice at end of bloodshed and death of Hitler,

The surrender of Hitler's generals on May 8, 1945 was greeted with unbounded relief by all the peoples of the world, including the German people, who had lost 2,850,000 of their sons on the battlefield. Everywhere the end of the European carnage gave human beings a radiant moment to express their truest feelings and deepest aspirations. In that moment, "enemy" disappeared from the human tongue. In the streets of Germany's shattered cities, American soldiers gave their chocolate bars to chil-

dren. In the concentration camp at Salzwedel, a seventeen-year-old Jewish girl from Budapest handed the cigarette she had just received from a GI to a German prisoner who had been her guard a few days before. In the barracks of the V-bomb plant at Fallersleben, Polish, Russian, Yugoslav, French and Italian workers blended their languages and songs, and spoke with indomitable hope of the future. In the nearby prisoner of war camp, German combat veterans threw away their insignia and opened

their frayed Wehrmacht tunics to the sunlight. In the wrecked factory at Hoechst, near Frankfurt, old Social Democratic and Catholic trade unionists, newly released from Nazi concentration camps, elected shop councils, repaired their tools, and went back to work. In Trafalgar Square and the Place de la Concorde, soldiers and civilians of all nations celebrated. In Moscow, a few weeks before, Russians had mourned the death of Franklin D. Roosevelt. Now, on V-E Day, at word that the war had ended

RECONSTRUCTION of Stalingrad began before the war was over. Damage to Russian cities was vast; shortages of construction materials were partly met by grants from the United Nations Relief and Rehabilitation Administration. From 1943 through 1949, UNRRA contributed $249,000,000 toward rebuilding the Soviet Union's razed areas.

STALIN promised at Potsdam in July-August 1945 that there would be civil liberty, free elections and representative governments in countries occupied by the Soviets. He is shown in white uniform, with Molotov and Vishinsky at his left. For the U. S. and Britain, Harry S. Truman and Clement Attlee had replaced Roosevelt and Churchill.

TO EXPRESS THEIR PRO-WESTERN FEELINGS

as democratic spirit unites all

at last—the war which had cost Russia 7,500,000 soldiers and untold civilians— Moscow became delirious. Emotion-filled crowds embraced American and British soldiers in loving brotherhood. "This outburst of affection for foreigners was full of tragedy as well as joy," wrote an American witness, "for it symbolized for the Russian people the deepest meaning of the wartime partnership—the hope that . . . isolation and fear and suspicion were ending and that they might henceforth live in comradeship with . . . the world."

REHABILITATION aid to the scorched-earth areas of Russia included food processing equipment, seed and tractors. The Kremlin later tried to disparage both lend-lease and UNRRA aid, but an American observer reported that the Russians preferred to believe the evidence of their eyes. Above, farmers examine bean seed sacks from Cincinnati.

INMATES of the Nordhausen camp were compelled to work underground in a munitions plant. Brutality, starvation and exhaustion killed 20,000 here; American troops found 3000 of them still unburied. Emergency aid saved many victims; to others it came late.

COWS graze by the bunker behind Berlin's New Chancellery, where Hitler committed suicide a few days before the close of the war.

THE HARVEST of Nazism

The sick mind of Adolf Hitler dreamed of an empire that would last a thousand years. Instead, his brief rule laid waste the monuments of a thousand years of German creative effort—of the great cities identified for centuries with the finest achievements of German culture, only Heidelberg stood intact. The German spirit suffered even greater ravages. Hitler had made science, industry and politics his accomplices, and in so doing, had caused the angry and the thoughtless to forget that beneath the soulless Reich of the Gestapo, the Nazi General Staff, Krupp, and the SS, still lived the universal Germany of Bach, Kant, Schiller, Beethoven, Brahms, Goethe and Heine. That Germany now struggled to climb from the rubble and rejoin the world.

NUREMBERG, whose old inner city was one of the finest examples of Gothic architecture in Germany, was reduced to this by Hitler's war.

Under Nazism, the city had been the site for Party Congresses. Later, the major Nazi war criminals were tried and hanged here.

ATOMIC BLASTS over Hiroshima and Nagasaki (above) brought the war to an apocalyptic end. Although Japan's main cities had already been crippled by saturation bombing and incendiary raids, the military refused to surrender. On August 6, 1945, a B-29 dropped an atom bomb on Hiroshima. On the 8th, the Soviet Army invaded Japanese-occupied Manchuria. On the 9th, a second bomb fell on Nagasaki. On the 10th, Tokyo announced that the Emperor would accept Allied terms. The delay cost more than 100,000 people their lives.

114

PEACE news was received with frenzied joy by the Chinese people, who had been suffering war and civil war for decades. This is how Chungking reacted to the war's end.

WORLD celebrates end of the war,
but atomic bombs deliver apocalyptic warning

The surrender of Imperial Japan on August 14, 1945 ended the second world war. The fighting in China and on the islands of the Western Pacific had inflicted cruel casualties on all the main belligerents. Civilian losses in China ran into uncounted millions; Japan lost more than 1,500,000 soldiers and more than 400,000 civilians. The road from Bataan to Tokyo cost the U. S. 300,000 killed and wounded; British and Australian losses were comparable. But all the bloodshed and violence seemed ended as the Japanese armies on the Chinese mainland laid down their arms, and as Allied forces quietly occupied the main islands of Japan. As in Europe, the main war criminals were brought to trial and executed. V-J Day offered the peoples of the Orient their first promise of general peace since 1931, when Japan invaded Manchuria. Independence was on the horizon for India, Pakistan, Burma and Indonesia. Asia looked to that horizon with hope.

RITUAL of surrender took place aboard the battleship Missouri in Tokyo Bay on September 2, 1945. Japan gave up all her conquests since the 1895 war against China.

NEW YORK felt the same way as Chungking about the news that peace had come. To the women and children on the fire-escape of this tenement in the East Side's "Little Italy," V-J Day meant the return from overseas of their sons, husbands, brothers and fathers.

115

SUCCESSES BY SURPRISE ATTACK (LIKE PEARL HARBOR ABOVE) DID NOT BRING AXIS VICTORY, BUT ALLIED VICTORY BY ARMS ALONE (LIKE

NO PEACE is possible, world soon learns, when military victory fails to secure

To safeguard peace, a United Nations organization was set up under a Charter adopted at San Francisco on June 25, 1945. It stated, "We, the peoples of the United Nations, determined to save succeeding generations from the scourge of war, which twice in our lifetime has brought sorrow to mankind, and to reaffirm our faith in fundamental human

rights, in the dignity and worth of the human person . . . do hereby establish an international organization to be known as the United Nations." Despite the common longings of all peoples, the Charter did not bring peace. Although the world had paid 20,000,000 lives to destroy one totalitarian tyranny, another was seated securely at the San Francisco conference

table. The Communist leaders, who had discarded "fundamental human rights" in November 1917 and had employed against the Russian people the same methods for which the major Nazi leaders were hanged at Nuremberg, had not made peace with the people they ruled or with the world. Stalin aided Hitler from September 1939 to June 22, 1941.

THE SINKING OF JAPAN'S WARSHIPS ABOVE) DID NOT BRING PEACE, BECAUSE A VAST PORTION OF THE HUMAN RACE STILL REMAINED ENSLAVED

fundamental human rights, and Communists stick to their program

The Nazi invasion forced him to seek help from the Russian people and the non-Communist world, and he had given lip service to freedom to win favor at home and abroad, but his program was unchanged. His only true allies were the leaders of the nominally dissolved Communist International, and his major war aim was to bring them to power. In support of their common cause, he used or withheld Soviet troops, encouraged or balked Britain and America, was conciliatory or intransigent. He kept the vow he had taken at Lenin's funeral to "strengthen and expand the Communist International." He did so even during his war with Hitler. But the world soon knew what Stalin had been plotting since 1941.

STALIN knew that war was only the continuation of politics.

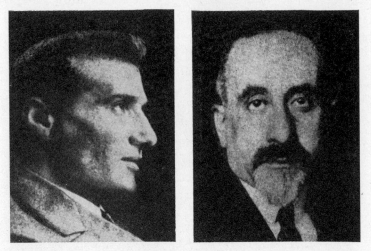

HENRYK ERLICH (right) and Victor Alter were respected Polish labor leaders; in 1917, Erlich had represented the Jewish Socialist Bund in the Petrograd Soviet. In September 1939, when the Soviets occupied East Poland, they were arrested and imprisoned in the U.S.S.R.

TWO SOCIALISTS DIE

After two years in Soviet prisons, Erlich and Alter were sentenced to death for "collaboration with the fascists" in July 1941. But following the Soviet-Polish agreement, they were released, and the Soviets then urged them to form a non-partisan world Jewish anti-Hitler committee. They agreed, and outlined their plans to Stalin. In December 1941, they disappeared. After numerous queries by Mrs. Roosevelt, William Green and others, Soviet Ambassador Litvinov announced that they had been shot in December 1942 as Nazi agents.

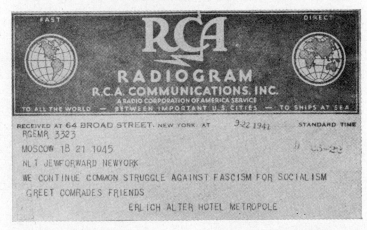

"FREED" in September 1941, Erlich and Alter cabled this message on October 22 from Moscow to the *Jewish Daily Forward*, in New York.

REMAINS of a Polish major were exhumed at Katyn. Among the dead were engineers, professors and other reservists mobilized in 1939.

THIS KATYN VICTIM'S HANDS WERE TIED TIGHTLY BEHIND HIS BACK

POLISH labor leaders and officers

On July 30, 1941, the Kremlin agreed to the formation of a Polish army on Soviet soil and to the release of the 181,000 Polish war prisoners, including 10,000 officers, whom the Soviets had captured in 1939. When fewer than 400 officers reported, the Polish government made inquiries of the Kremlin; it made four in the next several months; all were futile. On April 13, 1943, Berlin announced that mass graves containing "about 10,000 Polish officers" had been found in the Katyn forest, near Smolensk, Russia. Berlin charged that the officers had been killed by the NKVD in 1940. Moscow soon retorted that the

THE POLISH GOVERNMENT'S REQUEST FOR AN INVESTIGATION GAVE STALIN A PRETEXT TO SEVER RELATIONS AND SPONSOR A PUPPET REGIME

are murdered by the NKVD during the war, to soften up the country for Communist dictatorship

forest was an ancient burial ground. On the 16th, a Polish minister asked for an impartial investigation by the Red Cross. The Kremlin labeled his appeal "direct assistance to the enemy in the fabrication of a foul lie," and on the 25th, severed relations with the Polish government. Meanwhile, the Germans sent an international panel of doctors and scientists to Katyn. On the 30th, the panel concluded that the NKVD was responsible. It reported that only 4253 bodies had been found; that no documents on the bodies were dated later than May 1940—more than a year before the Soviets evacuated Smolensk; that spruce trees on the graves had been planted sometime in 1940; and that the men had been shot with German-made revolvers of a type exported to the U.S.S.R. between 1922 and 1931. When Soviet troops reentered Katyn in 1944, services were held for the "11,000 victims of fascism," but the bodies were not re-exhumed to refute the panel's verdict. The Soviet prosecutor at the main Nuremberg trial indicted the Nazis for killing "11,000 Polish officers" at Katyn. But the Nazi leaders, guilty of so many other mass murders, were acquitted of the murder of the 4253 Polish officers. No trace of the other 6000 has been found to this day.

WEAPONS were parachuted to Warsaw rebels during the uprising (August 1-October 2, 1944) by RAF Liberators with Polish, British and South African suicide crews. Soviet airstrips were barred to U. S. pilots until September; on the 18th, 104 U. S. planes aided Warsaw.

WARSAW uprising, betrayed

The Polish request for an investigation of Katyn gave Stalin a convenient pretext to break off relations with the Polish Government-in-exile and to groom a Polish Communist group to take over the country. The Polish Government continued its efforts to restore relations, however, and on July 30, 1944, with Soviet forces under Marshal Rokossovsky approaching Warsaw, Polish Premier Stanislaw Mikolajczyk went to Moscow. The night before, Soviet artillery had closed within range of Praga, an industrial suburb of Warsaw, and Radio Moscow's Polish-language broadcast proclaimed at 8:15 P. M., "No doubt Warsaw already hears the guns of the battle that is soon to bring her liberation. . . . The hour of action has already arrived. . . . By direct active struggle in the streets of Warsaw, in its houses, factories and stores, we not only hasten the moment of final liberation, but also save the nation's property and the lives of our brethren. Poles, the time of liberation is at hand! Poles, to arms! There is not a moment to lose!" Three days later, the people of Warsaw rose and attacked the five German divisions in the city, soon reinforced by three others. On the night of August 3, Mikolajczyk asked Stalin for aid to the Warsaw insurgents, but was told, "We hope to take Warsaw on August 5 or 6, but the Germans are defending it more savagely than we expected. There will be a small delay in capturing the city." Stalin advised him instead to take the matter up with the Polish Communist group. On the 6th, Mikolajczyk showed Stalin a message from Colonel Kalugin of the Red Army, which said, "Marshal Comrade Stalin: I am in personal contact with the commander of Warsaw garrison, who is leading heroic partisan fight of nation

JUDGE who tried sixteen Polish underground leaders for "sabotage," June 1-4, 1945, was V. V. Ulrich (extreme left), who had presided at the trials of the Old Bolsheviks in the same Moscow courtroom in 1936-38. Fifteen of the sixteen Polish defendants "confessed."

DEFENDANTS at the trial of the sixteen Polish underground leaders received light sentences, although they were convicted of "drawing up plans for military action in a block with Germany against the U.S.S.R." They had been invited to Moscow to help organize the new

by Stalin, further weakens democratic forces

against Hitler bandits. . . . The heroic population of Warsaw trusts that in a few hours time you will give them armed support." Stalin read the message and said, "I don't know this man Kalugin. I'll inquire about him. And I'll still do my best to help Warsaw. The Germans are more difficult than we expected." On the 11th, Warsaw pleaded, "German tanks accompanied by artillery fire from armored trains, mortars, grenades and anti-tank guns. Enormous overwhelming superiority of enemy fire." While Soviet troops paused outside the city, Tass, the Soviet news agency, announced that "the London Polish sources responsible for the Warsaw uprising made no attempt to coordinate the revolt with the Soviet High Command. The responsibility for the Warsaw events thus lies with the Polish emigré circles in London." As RAF, and later American, planes began to parachute food and weapons to the Warsaw rebels, Stalin wired Mikolajczyk, "I have become convinced that the Warsaw action, which was undertaken without the knowledge of the Soviet command, is a thoughtless adventure causing unnecessary losses among the inhabitants. . . . In view of this state of affairs, the Soviet command cuts itself away from the Warsaw adventure and cannot take any responsibility for it." On October 2, two months after the Polish underground forces had been summoned to arms by Radio Moscow, they finally surrendered. When the uprising started, Warsaw's population was 1,000,000. When the sixty-three-day battle was over, 250,000 were dead, wounded or missing. The Red Army entered the ruined city on January 17, a few weeks after Stalin recognized his Communist committee as the "Provisional Government of Liberated Democratic Poland."

PUPPET "Union of Polish Patriots" was set up by the Kremlin in 1941, later revamped as the "Committee of National Liberation," and recognized by Stalin in December 1944. Here he signs a treaty with the group, led by Communist Boleslaw Bierut at the extreme right.

"Polish Government of National Unity" in March 1945, but instead were placed under arrest. When one defendant, Zbigniew Stypulkowski, pleaded "not guilty" and insisted he had come to Moscow at the invitation of a Soviet officer, Judge Ulrich replied: "I am afraid you became an easy victim of an NKVD trick." Despite the court's apparent leniency, only two of the defendants were alive and free six years later. Three of them are known to be dead, and the other eleven are still in Soviet jails. Judge Ulrich died in Moscow in 1951.

BREAD made from UNRRA-supplied wheat was a major part of Poland's diet in 1946. UNRRA aid ($474,500,000) amounted to a dollar a day for each person in Poland. Above, Wincenty Rakowski starts home with two loaves, the basic daily ration for his family of six.

COALITION of Communists
and democrats promises a free election in 1945

When America and Britain insisted on the rights of the Polish democratic parties and the Government-in-exile, Stalin agreed at the Yalta conference in February 1945 that his Communist "Provisional Government now functioning in Poland should . . . be reorganized on a broader democratic basis with the inclusion of democratic leaders from Poland itself and from Poles abroad. This new Government of National Unity . . . should be pledged to the holding of free and unfettered elections as soon as possible on the basis of universal suffrage and the secret ballot." The new coalition government was set up shortly after the trial of the sixteen underground leaders in June. The President was Boleslaw Bierut, a veteran Communist; the Premier was Edward Osobka-Morawski, a former clerk and head of the Communist-controlled Polish "Socialist" Party; the First Deputy Premier was Wladislaw Gomulka, General Secretary of the Communist Party. Mikolajczyk, head of the Peasant Party, Poland's largest, was named Second Deputy Premier and Minister of Agriculture, but fourteen of the twenty cabinet posts, including the important Ministries of the Interior and Public Security, were in Communist hands. A new agreement, signed in Moscow, provided that all parties in the coalition were to have "full freedom of organizational work, freedom of assembly, press and propaganda," and announced that elections would be held by "universal, equal, direct and secret ballot . . . possibly before the end of 1945."

HEIFERS at Gdansk harbor were sent by UNRRA. Farmers in Ohio, Maryland, Pennsylvania, Michigan, Indiana, Illinois, Iowa and Oregon donated 150. When UNRRA aid ceased, Communists said the U.S. was trying "to make slaves of our people through starvation."

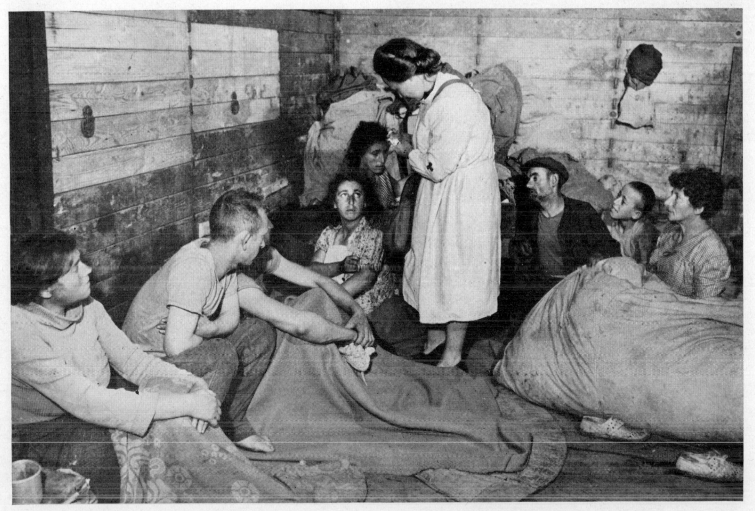

BOX CARS brought back some of the 1,500,000 Poles who had been deported to the U.S.S.R. in 1939. Most of them had spent years in forced labor camps, and many possessed documentary evidence of the huge Soviet slave labor system. This train returned in July 1946.

PRINTING plant of the Peasant Party was raided by Communists before the January 1947 election. The presses were damaged and pamphlets destroyed. Said Communist Premier Osobka-Morawski: "The Government cannot and will not allow the elections to be lost."

VOTING in the 1947 election (above) was open, with government ballots (Number 3) larger than those of other parties'. Many voters showed Communist ballots to the guards but voted anti-Communist with concealed ballots. Below, Communist headquarters in Warsaw.

RULING Poland today is Communist Boleslaw Bierut, an agent of Beria's NKVD in 1939.

FRAUD at 1947 election drives out democrats; Party terror installs police state

The Communists had little hope of winning a free election in Poland, and soon after the coalition government reached Warsaw, the Communist security police began a campaign of terror against the peasants and the leaders of Mikolajczyk's Peasant Party. Stalin had told his Polish comrades that the election, finally slated for January 19, 1947, "must be won before the election." By December 1, 1946, 670 members of the Peasant Party's local executive committees, 147 members of district committees, seven members of provincial committees, and twenty-two members of its supreme council were in jail. Just before the election, another 100,000 members were arrested, and their candidates stricken from the ballot in ten districts (where a fourth of the population lived). On the eve of the election, the Communists sent identical telegrams to thousands of Peasant Party officials: "Mikolajczyk killed last night in plane accident," signed "General Secretary, Polish Peasant Party." Despite such tactics, the Peasant Party won from 65 to 85 per cent of the votes in the thirty-three polling places where there was a public count; it estimated its actual vote at 74 per cent. The government credited it with only 8 per cent, however, and a few months later, Mikolajczyk was forced to flee. The Polish Communist regime has outlawed strikes, frozen workers to their jobs, destroyed cooperatives, begun to collectivize the land, and undertaken purges of dissidents and army officers. As in Russia, terror rules.

RETURNING Soviet Marshal Konstantin Rokossovsky, named Poland's Minister of Defense in 1949, had marked time outside Warsaw in 1944 while the underground was being destroyed. Soviet forces in Poland are aided by 230,000 Polish security police and 120,000 militiamen.

IMPROVING on reality was the aim of this Polish photographer, who set up his own pretty backdrop to keep the ruins out of his picture. →

WOODEN CROSS in potter's field marks the grave of Nikola Petkov, Bulgarian Peasant leader executed by Dimitrov's Communist regime.

DIMITROV (right) and Yugoslav dictator Tito favored a federation of Balkan Communist states in 1947, but the Kremlin said "No."

THE END OF GEORGI DIMITROV

Georgi Dimitrov, who had been Stalin's spokesman at the Comintern's Trojan Horse Congress in 1935, warned the Bulgarian people after Petkov's execution that all active opponents of Communism could expect the same fate. However, when Dimitrov proposed to Marshal Tito that the Balkan Communist states unite, the Kremlin forced him to retract, and his fortunes began to decline. His health did also. Early in 1949, he went to Moscow for medical treatment. When he died there on July 2, 1949, he received an elaborate state funeral.

CHERVENKOV, the new Bulgarian chief, leads Dimitrov's pallbearers, followed by Voroshilov. Also present: Stalin, Beria and Malenkov.

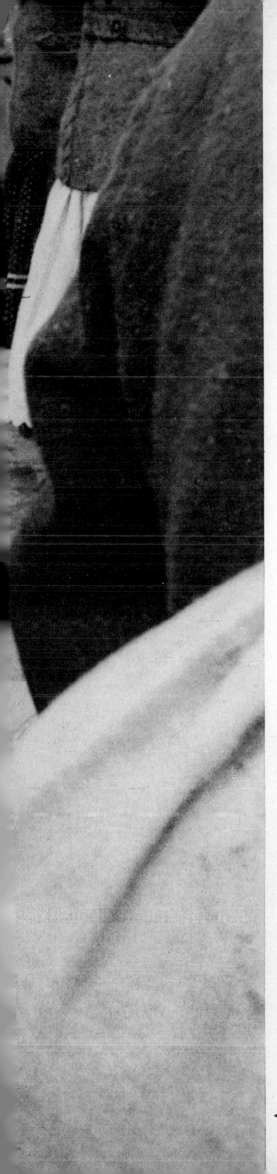

OLD WARHORSES of the Comintern

follow Vishinsky and the Soviet Army into Rumania and Bulgaria

When Soviet troops entered Rumania in August 1944, King Michael directed a coup d'etat which overthrew pro-Nazi General Antonescu's cabinet and accepted armistice terms. The new government did not satisfy Stalin. In March 1945, he sent Andrei Vishinsky (then Vice-Minister of Foreign Affairs) to Bucharest, where he forced King Michael to name a pro-Communist cabinet. Additional Communist pressure compelled Michael to abdicate, on December 30, 1947. A Communist constitution was adopted a few months later, and all opposition groups crushed. Through Soviet-controlled joint companies covering the main industries and resources, the Kremlin obtained an economic stranglehold. The pattern was similar in Bulgaria, where the pro-Axis government had been replaced in 1944 by a new cabinet including Nikola Mushanov, a veteran democrat. This government was removed when the Soviet Army occupied the country and was replaced by a Communist-dominated "Fatherland Front" which included the fascist Demian Veltchev. Mushanov, whom Radio Moscow had once called "the conscience of Bulgaria," died in a Communist jail in 1951. A rigged election, boycotted by the democratic Peasant Party, put the Fatherland Front in control in November 1945. New balloting in October 1946 gave the Peasant and Social Democratic parties 101 of the 465 seats in Parliament, but the Communist regime, headed by Georgi Dimitrov and Vassil Kolarov, staged a series of "treason" trials, which culminated in

the execution in September 1947 of Nikola Petkov, the Peasant Party's leader. The Communists then expelled the Opposition parties from Parliament and silenced their press. In 1949, they seized direct control of government agencies, the army, militia and police. That November,

ANA PAUKER, Rumania's Vice-Premier and Foreign Minister, is a present Communist luminary. Vishinsky at the 1938 Moscow trial branded her late husband a "traitor."

Traicho Kostov, the Party's General Secretary and author of the 1947 constitution, was tried for alleged "left sectarian Trotskyite deviation" back in 1933, was accused of being a British and Yugoslav agent, and was hanged on December 16. Kolarov died shortly afterwards. Vulko Chervenkov has been dictator ever since.

VETERAN of Rumania's war of independence in 1877 converses with a distinguished visitor and fellow soldier, Soviet Marshal Voroshilov.

WILSON inspired Czech Declaration of Independence of 1918, which states, "We accept the American principles as laid down by President Wilson; the principles of liberated mankind—of the actual equality of nations—and of governments deriving all their just power from the consent of the governed." Right, Thomas Masaryk in Prague.

CZECHOSLOVAKIA, Central Europe's freest republic for twenty years,

ROOSEVELT gave the Czechoslovak Government-in-exile, headed by Benes, lend-lease in July 1941 and full recognition that October. The two are shown in 1943, in Washington.

The Republic of Czechoslovakia was the freest country in Central Europe from its birth in 1918 until its death in 1938-39. The father of its freedom, and its president until 1935, was Professor Thomas G. Masaryk, a Wilsonian democrat who regarded the first great war as a struggle between humanitarian and autocratic principles. His ideals were incorporated in the 1920 constitution—the only democratic charter east of the Rhine to survive intact during the twenty-year armistice. No country did more than Czechoslovakia to further the cultural development of its nationalities; its Sudeten Germans, Hungarians, Poles and other groups ran schools and courts in their own languages and sent deputies to Parliament. One of the new republic's first acts was to distribute large estates, thereby creating over half a million new farmers. Czechoslovakia's social insurance system became the model for France and several Latin American countries. Small business was encouraged; only 2 per cent of industrial enterprises employed more than twenty persons. Many industries were linked with agricultural cooperatives; a great network of consumers' cooperatives served 886,000 people. (The German minority had its own central cooperative association.) Practi-

PRAGUE civilians fought Nazi SS troops on the barricades in April 1945, as American and Soviet armies drove toward Czechoslovakia. General Vlasov's Russian anti-Stalin forces joined in the battle against the SS men. President Benes returned to the capital on May 16.

JOINT PARADE of Soviet troops and General Patton's Third Army took place in Pilsen, Czechoslovakia, after its capture by the Americans on May 6, 1945. Allied Supreme Headquarters instructed Patton's onrushing armored forces not to cross the Karlsbad-Pilsen line, al-

BENES (above left) sought support during the Munich crisis from Soviet Foreign Commissar Litvinov (above right), who promised that the Kremlin would fulfill its pact with Czechoslovakia if France gave Prague military aid. Left, Sudeten Germans raise the swastika in Brunn, March 1939, to celebrate the end of the Czechoslovak Republic.

tries to build a bridge of understanding between the western democracies and the Stalin regime

cally all workers belonged to trade unions; there were labor courts, and the work week was limited to forty-eight hours. When Masaryk resigned at the age of 85, he said, "Remember that states can be maintained only by respecting those ideals which brought them into being." His successor, Dr. Eduard Benes, developed close relations with France and distinguished himself in the League of Nations as a spokesman for collective security. The rise of Hitler, together with the slump of the Sudetenland industries in the world depression, encouraged Konrad Henlein's pro-Nazi Sudeten German Party, which in 1935 won forty-five of

the seventy-two German seats in Parliament. Henlein professed allegiance to the republic, but plotted with Berlin to destroy it. As Hitler stepped up his attacks on Benes, Henlein provoked clashes between Czechs and Germans until Munich gave the Sudeten areas to Nazi Germany. Benes took refuge in London and after the defeat of France was recognized as head of the Czechoslovak Provisional Government. Munich helped convince Benes that the future of his country depended on his ability to get along with Stalin. In 1945, he agreed to cede him the Carpatho-Ukrainian region, in the hope of forestalling any future friction.

STALIN signed a "friendship, mutual assistance and postwar collaboration" treaty with Benes in Moscow in December 1943. Soviet President Kalinin is shaking Benes's hand.

though there was little organized German resistance in Western Czechoslovakia, and Patton could have easily pushed on to Prague. The Communist Party subsequently made political capital of the fact that the Soviet Army was the first to enter the embattled city.

COMMUNIST POSTER at the May Day Parade in Prague, 1946, displayed this benign portrait of Stalin. During 1946 and 1947, the local Communists used two themes to win popular support; they harped on the Munich pact and demanded the expulsion of the Sudeten Germans.

SUICIDE

Communist squads take over and force a new constitution

Czechoslovakia's first postwar cabinet included four Communists. During 1945 and 1946, the Communists quietly took over key posts in the trade unions, army and police. Although the Party polled only about one-third of the vote in the free election of May 1946, Comintern veteran Klement Gottwald became Premier, and another Communist was named Minister of the Interior. Benes remained president, however, and since civil liberties were not immediately suppressed, sympathizers abroad argued that, because of Czechoslovakia's strong pro-western traditions, she would become the first "democratic Communist" state. This theory was exploded in February 1948, when Communist "action squads," operating under the guidance of Soviet envoy Zorin, staged a coup d'état and seized the headquarters of the opposition parties. On March 10, Foreign Minister Jan Masaryk, son of the republic's first president and for many years an advocate of close relations with the Kremlin, leaped to his death from the window of Czernin Palace, Prague. His successor was Dr. Vladimir Clementis, a leading Communist who was later purged. That May brought a new constitution which drastically curtailed freedom. May 30 offered the electorate a single Communist-dominated slate of candidates for a new National Assembly. Despite heavy pressure, President Benes on June 7, 1948 refused to sign the new constitution and resigned. A week later, Gottwald became president, and the Communists were given twelve posts, a majority, in his cabinet. On June 25, they absorbed the Social Democrats.

JAN MASARYK (left) looked like this at his last public appearance, two days before he killed himself. Above, his funeral cortège passes the statue of St. Wenceslas, Prague.

BENES argued warmly, but Communist Premier Gottwald listened coldly, after the coup of February 1948. Here Benes (right) has just been handed Gottwald's cabinet list.

PRAGUE
mourns the passing of an era

Totalitarian measures followed fast on Benes's death. In October 1948, forced labor camps were introduced, and the security police was authorized to arrest citizens for anything from coming late to work to alleged "conspiracy against the state." By January, the political police had been put on a military footing and trial by jury abolished. The teachings of Thomas Masaryk were erased from textbooks. A "Ministry of Information and Enlightenment" began indoctrinating the public in Communism. Special Party schools were set up to retrain civil servants for the newest Communist state.

GOTTWALD and his wife reviewed a parade of the patriotic Sokol sports association in the summer of 1948. The popular ovation which the marchers gave Truhlar (saluting), veteran head of the Sokol, did not please the Communist dictator. The Sokol, and all other such Czech organizations, have long since come under Communist control.

BENES died on September 3, 1948 and lay in state at his home. So greatly did the public reverence him, the Communists dared not deny his body a solemn state funeral.

COMINFORM (Communist Information Bureau, left) met in Prague in 1949. Twenty-nine Communist parties sent delegates to this largest international Communist meeting since the "Trojan Horse Congress" of 1935. The Cominform was secretly organized in Poland in 1947, to succeed the Comintern, "dissolved" four years earlier.

PRAGUE's populace knelt and wept (right) when the Benes funeral procession passed. He had been the last living symbol of the humane state created by Thomas Masaryk.

BLACK MARKET patrons in Budapest stopped to watch this performance in the spring of 1946. The acrobats hoped to earn enough to eat.

HUNGER SENT THESE PEOPLE OUT OF BUDAPEST IN SEARCH FOR FOOD;

HUNGARY votes for agrarian

Between the two world wars, Hungary was a semi-feudal state ruled by a regent, Admiral Horthy. Communist terror in 1919 had been followed immediately by White terror. Horthy had then established a relatively stable regime, but thirty-six great estate holders kept over a million acres of land, while 1,200,000 peasants had to subsist on 950,000 acres. Nevertheless, there was parliamentary opposition and a trade union movement in the country until the period of Nazi domination. As an Axis partner, Hungary paid a high price; she lost ten divisions on the Stalingrad front. In October 1944, as the Soviet Army moved in, Horthy announced that he would accept Allied surrender terms; however, he was seized by the Germans, who installed in power the pro-Nazi Arrow Cross. Its reign of terror rivaled Hitler's. After V-E Day, an Allied Control Commission, headed by Marshal Voroshilov, was set up in Budapest to give the Hungarian people the democratic rights promised to them at Yalta and Potsdam. Early in 1945, the large estates were distributed among the peasants. Meanwhile, the Communist Party, which dominated the "clearance committees" charged with eliminating pro-Nazis from public life, was recruiting former Arrow Cross members by promising them immunity from prosecution as war criminals. At the same time, the Soviet authorities were dismantling plants as reparations and seizing key industries which Nazi corporations had taken over during the war. The Kremlin thus obtained control of Hungary's railway system, its largest coal mines, 40 per cent of its bauxite, and other important assets. In the compara-

CATTLE REQUISITIONING TO FEED THE SOVIET ARMY CAUSED FAMINE

liberals, but Nazis help Communists to power

tively free election on November 4, 1945, the moderate Small-holders Party obtained a majority. Smallholder Ferenc Nagy became Prime Minister, but he was forced to accept one of the Comintern leaders, Matyas Rakosi, as Vice-Premier and to name a Communist Minister of the Interior. In April 1946, Stalin received Nagy's cabinet in Moscow and drank toasts to Soviet-Hungarian friendship. Inside Hungary, however, the Interior Ministry began arresting key members of Nagy's party as "conspirators against the state," and deporting members of the German minority who had lived in Hungary for centuries, though it granted exemptions to former Nazis and Arrow Cross members who agreed to join the Communist Party. By May 1947, the Communists were strong enough to drive Nagy from office. Elections in August, held under a reign of terror, gave the Communist-dominated "Independence Front" the largest bloc of seats. Soon after, the opposition parties were completely ousted from parliament. In June 1948, Smallholder Zoltan Tildy was forced out as president; in July, the Communists absorbed the Social Democrats. A totalitarian constitution was adopted on August 18, 1949. Next, the Communist regime introduced forcible collectivization, but met strong resistance. In the spring of 1951, it began to deport peasants branded as "kulaks." It also started to move political "undesirables" out of cities, under the Arrow Cross law of 1944 for the transport of Jews to Nazi extermination camps. Similar deportations were taking place at the same time in Communist Czechoslovakia and Communist Rumania.

CARDINAL MINDSZENTY, jailed in 1944 by the Hungarian Nazis and condemned to penal servitude for life by a Communist court in 1949 after an extorted confession, remains a symbol of resistance. Before his arrest, he had said, "History tells us that everything on this earth is transitory, be it the work of Genghis Khan or Hitler. God sends to peoples a lash and many sufferings; but when the cold hand of death touches them, millions of peoples and nations sigh in relief." Above, in court, after forty days of Communist torture.

MATYAS RAKOSI (left), General Secretary of the Communist Party, is the present dictator of Hungary. Under Horthy, he spent fifteen years in prison before being released to the Kremlin in exchange for Hungarian war prisoners. Laszlo Rajk (right), late Communist Minister of Interior and Foreign Affairs, was tried on charges of having been a lifelong Horthy agent; of subverting the International Brigade in Spain; of plotting to kill his comrades. He "confessed" and asked to be hanged. On October 15, 1949 his request was granted.

COMMUNISTS armed with brass knuckles, rubber hose, and hatchet-like *fokos* broke up this opposition meeting in June 1947 in Szeged.

BRITISH forces were warmly welcomed when they liberated Athens on October 13, 1944; the kiss was for Flight Lt. F. Flude, of Balham.

MARKOS VIFIADES (left) led the Greek Communist guerrillas until February 1949, when it was announced that he had been "seriously ill" for some time. His present whereabouts are unknown. Nicholas Zachariades (right), the Party's general secretary, succeeded him.

GREECE fights back and routs
Communist army after four years of civil war

During the three and a half years of Nazi occupation, Greece had less food than any other nation in Europe. When it was liberated in 1944, it was starved and desolate. Its recovery was further impeded that December, when Communist armed forces made a bid for power. Repulsed by loyalist troops, the Communists retired to the hills and waged guerrilla war for almost four years, aided by weapons and supplies from Soviet-dominated Albania, Yugoslavia and Bulgaria to the north. The United Nations supervised democratic elections in March 1946, but the Communists boycotted them and continued to fight. With the withdrawal of the British forces which had helped in the liberation, the United States extended military aid. This program, announced on March 12, 1947, became known as the Truman Doctrine. American supplies and military advice enabled the Greek Army to take the offensive, and on October 16, 1949, the Athens government announced the end of the civil war. Elections the following spring resulted in a victory for moderates and socialists. Sophocles Venizelos, son of the premier who brought Greece into World War I against Imperial Germany, became prime minister on September 11, 1950. His Liberal Party has been dominant in the democratic coalitions which have governed Greece ever since. Although economic recovery has not been easy, the Greeks—thanks to effective American and United Nations aid—are the only Balkan people today who enjoy any democratic freedom.

HOMELESS children at a camp in Ioannina sang while awaiting their rations of powdered milk, supplied by a United Nations relief team.

WIDOWS in Athens mourn for their husbands, slain during the civil war. It lasted four years and cost Greece enormous casualties.

SUPPLIES like these guns at Konnitsa were given the Greek Army under the Truman Doctrine. The U. S. also sent a military mission.

COMMUNIST GUERRILLAS tried to seize power in Athens on December 2, 1944. Above, four of them, well armed, take part in an attack on police headquarters. The initials K.K.E. stand for "Komounistikó Kómma Ellados"—"Communist Party of Greece." Its emblem is plain.

MARSHALL PLAN aid to France, totaling more than a billion dollars, helped production rise above pre-war levels. The plan was launched by sixteen nations in Paris on September 7, 1947. On October 22, Andrei Zhdanov, of the Soviet Politburo, formally called on Commu- nists the world over to oppose it. In November, American citizens sent a "Friendship Train"—200 carloads of food—to France and Italy. Above, George Raoul Fremond, of Epieds, inspects his new tractor, obtained through the Marshall Plan, while his family looks on.

MINE STRIKE at St. Etienne, on October 20, 1948, was called by the Communist-controlled mine union. Above, strikers clash with Mobile Guards at the Villiers mine. Communists are still strong in steel, auto, aircraft, naval arsenal, transit and longshoremen's unions.

WRECK of the Paris to Arras express, derailed twelve miles south of Arras in 1947, killed twenty persons and injured forty others. The French National Railways announced that two lengths of track had been removed, and attributed the accident to Communist sabotage.

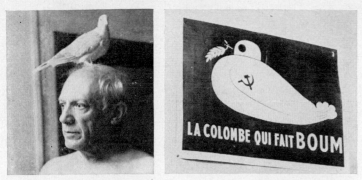

DOVE, designed by prominent artist Pablo Picasso (left), was the symbol of Communist "peace" propaganda. To counter this campaign, the non-partisan *Paix et Liberté*, founded by 38-year-old war hero Jean-Paul David, designed "The Dove That Goes Boom!"

FRANCE struggles with inflation;
Communists retain hold on labor, intellectuals

France's Communists, who had participated in the anti-Nazi resistance after Hitler attacked Russia, emerged from the war with a strong following among workers and intellectuals. After the war, they obtained the Defense Ministry and four other cabinet posts, with Maurice Thorez, their leader, as vice-premier. In 1946, they received 5,489,000 votes—more than any other party in France. When Premier Paul Ramadier expelled them from the cabinet in May 1947, they called a series of political strikes. That winter, they combined strikes with armed demonstrations, seizing temporary control of Marseilles, Nancy and other cities, but the disturbances were quelled by Socialist Interior Minister Jules Moch. Although anti-Communists have won about half the French workers into new unions, the Communists still hold a large segment of labor, partly because of the housing problem and very high living costs—many workers who earn ten times as much as they did before the war, pay prices twenty times as high for some consumers' goods. The Communists have used the ensuing discontent to attack the Marshall Plan, the Atlantic pact, and Foreign Minister Robert Schuman's planned merger of French, German, Italian, Belgian and Dutch coal and steel resources. While Communists have failed to stop French reconstruction, they remain a major force in politics.

ST. JUNIEN, a factory town in central France, renamed its central avenue for the Kremlin dictator, but Communists had to restore the name of Gambetta, a founder of the Third Republic, when the Minister of the Interior refused to deliver mail to Boulevard Staline.

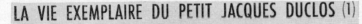

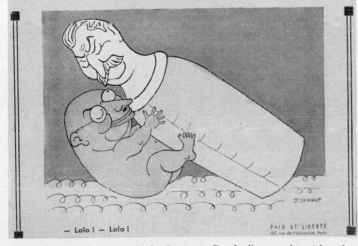

"THE EXEMPLARY LIFE of little Jacques Duclos" was the title of a *Paix et Liberté* poster series ridiculing the Communist leader. A letter from Duclos in 1946 gave U. S. Communists the signal to shift from advocating "unity" to an all-out fight against the government.

COMMUNIST leaders parade on May Day. Left to right, Marcel Cachin, who helped form the Party in 1919; Andre Marty, Moscow's favorite during the Popular Front of the thirties; Thorez, leader for twenty years until a recent illness; Duclos, delegate to the Cominform,

ITALY, burdened by overpopulation, peasant poverty, gives Party its biggest vote

Mussolini's war cost Italy 300,000 military casualties, heavy civilian losses, and priceless cultural and religious landmarks. At its end, farm production had fallen 40 per cent, industrial output 60 per cent; Italy was impoverished and dependent on foreign aid. Although American assistance through ECA has helped agriculture to regain pre-war levels and industry to surpass them, Italy's 47,000,000 people still face grave problems. About 1 per cent of the estate-holders own 22 per cent of the arable soil; 2,000,000 unemployed are a huge burden; and the annual population increase of 400,000 has not been met by emigration. Under these conditions, the Communists, led by the eloquent Palmiro Togliatti, have had a strong appeal. Expelled from the post-war coalition government in June 1947, they fomented crippling strikes in key industries, in an effort to oust Premier Alcide de Gasperi's Christian Democrats. The 1948 election was one of Italy's bitterest; despite parish-by-parish canvassing by the Catholic Action organization and a huge direct-mail from relatives in America, the Communists and their allies won 32 per cent of the vote. In municipal elections three years later, de Gasperi's party ousted them from many mayoralties, but their bloc polled 39 per cent of the vote—probably the strongest showing a Communist slate ever made in any free election. The same balloting recorded gains for the neo-fascist Social Movement Party. To reduce the tensions which have aided the Communists and fascists, the government has urged the division of 3,750,000 acres among landless peasants and has pressed other nations to absorb some of Italy's surplus workers. Both programs are moving slowly. The Communist Party has alienated some supporters by its opposition to American aid and Italian defense. In the spring of 1951, Defense Minister Rudolfo Pacciardi, who had led a Republican brigade in the Spanish Civil War, asked the Communists in the Chamber of Deputies whether they would fight for Italy in the event of Soviet attack. They shouted, *"Mai! Mai!"* (Never! Never!), but they failed to block passage of the government's defense budget. Nevertheless, Togliatti's Italian Communists, like Thorez' French, remain a powerful political factor in Western Europe.

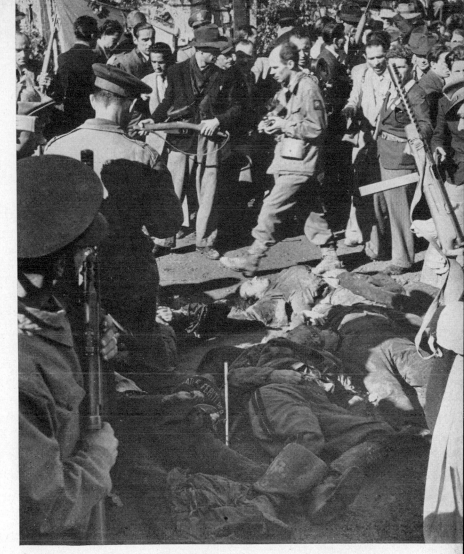

MUSSOLINI was seized by Italian partisans in the village of Dongo when the Nazis collapsed. The once-feared dictator and his mistress, Clara Petacci, were killed on April 28, 1945; their bodies were brought back to Milan and exhibited in a public square (above).

GARIBALDI, hero of Italian unification exploited by Communist election propaganda, talks back to Stalin in this anti-Communist poster used in the election of 1948.

ATTEMPT to kill Togliatti drew wire from Stalin (in *Pravda*, above) expressing "sadness that Togliatti's friends could not protect him from the treacherous attack."

ITALIAN COMMUNIST Party, third largest in the world, gains because Italy has, next to Spain, West Europe's lowest living standards. Above, a Party parade in Florence.

"HIS MASTER'S VOICE" is the title of this cartoon used in Italian election campaign. The little figure listening to Stalin is Togliatti, a Comintern leader since 1919.

SOVIET-WEHRMACHT relations were resumed in 1943, when Moscow set up the "League of German Officers" (above), led by captured General von Seydlitz and Bismarck's great-grandson, Heinrich von Einsiedel. The latter returned home, broke with the Party in 1948.

SIEGE of Berlin began when the Soviets ripped out its rail ties with West Germany at 6 A.M., June 24, then cut off West Berlin's power lines. At the time, the city had enough food for only thirty-six days. The enforced blackout lasted through the 1948-49 winter.

ANGLO-AMERICAN AIRLIFT DEFEATED STALIN'S STARVATION BLOCKADE

GERMANY is partitioned and

Stalin agreed at Potsdam that a four-power Allied Control Council, with headquarters in Berlin, would govern occupied Germany. The occupation's aims, he assented, were to punish war criminals, dismantle war industries, ban militarism, establish a democratic school and civil service system, and guarantee democratic elections, civil and religious freedom. Even before the Potsdam talks were over, the Soviets began to fill the Central Administration of their zone with German Communists and with Wehrmacht men who had served in the Moscow "League of German Officers." Soviet Military Government appointed Communists and officers to run the ministries of police, interior, education, propaganda and personnel. In Mecklenburg, sixty-four of the

CARGO PLANES LIKE THESE, CARRYING FLOUR, COAL, DEHYDRATED POTATOES AND CANNED MEAT, KEPT WEST BERLINERS ALIVE FOR TEN MONTHS

soon becomes Europe's toughest battleground

seventy-four mayors were Communists; in the twenty-six districts of Thuringia, twenty-three police chiefs and 75 per cent of the police officers held Party cards. In Berlin, Communists and Wehrmacht officers took over the key municipal jobs, the former Nazi radio station, and the ostensibly non-partisan *Berliner Zeitung*; Colonel Paul Markgraf, decorated by Hitler for his service at Stalingrad, became Berlin's chief of police. Shortly after the Communist coup in Prague, Stalin felt ready to try driving the western powers out of Berlin by a blockade. On June 24, 1948, the Soviet command cut off the city's railroad, motor and waterway ties with West Germany. About 2,500,000 Berliners faced this choice: starve, or surrender to Stalin.

COMMUNIST action squads broke into the Berlin Assembly, located in the Soviet sector, several times during the blockade; Communist police did not attempt to stop them, but Berlin's militant democratic leaders were not intimidated. Above, the riot of September 6.

BERLIN defies Stalin's blockade, inspires Germans and Soviet occupation troops

Stalin tried to conquer Berlin by blockade because other methods which had worked in the satellite states had failed here. American, British and French troops in West Berlin made all-out Communist terror impossible. The Berliners, though trapped behind the Iron Curtain, were far from fear-ridden; they took the offensive. In 1946, Berlin's workers had defied the Soviet demand that they merge with the Communists and instead had created a militant Social Democratic Party. In the City Council, located in the Soviet sector, Social Democrats like Ernst Reuter, Franz Neumann, Annedore Leber and Jeannette Wolff, supported by Liberals and Christian Democrats, had fought the MVD, Communist police chief Markgraf, and the Communist action squads who tried to break up the city government. Democratic elements had recaptured Berlin's unions, broken the power of the Communist "Cultural League," and set up a Free University. Berlin's courage had inspired many Soviet occupation troops to escape. It was this Berlin that Stalin now tried to strangle. The western powers replied with the airlift, and Berlin gave its own answer on September 9, 1948, when more than 250,000 of its citizens thronged to the Reichstag, on the dividing line between the British and Soviet sectors. They thronged although the British commandant, General Herbert, tried to bar the rally so as not to "provoke" the Kremlin. On the Reichstag steps, Franz Neumann cried out, "Berliners, do not forget that you not only defend your liberty, you also defend the freedom of those who long for it in the Soviet sector and Soviet zone! ... We greet all the peoples who love freedom." The rally closed with an old Austrian workers' song, *Brothers, Into the Sunlight of Freedom!* Soviet officers and men at their radio sets recognized its strains: it had been the revolutionary hymn of the People's Will Party. Moscow's barricades had heard it in 1905, and Petrograd's streets during the March 1917 Revolution, and a new anti-Stalin Russian version was even then circulating among occupation troops. On May 10, 1949, the blockade finally ended. Today democratic Berlin still defies the Kremlin and still inspires millions behind the Iron Curtain. Stalin knows to his frustration that he cannot take the city without starting World War III.

RUSSIAN OFFICERS watched Berlin fight Stalin; in March 1948, this one saw 50,000 people celebrate the centenary of the 1848 Revolution before the battered Reichstag. Despite the MVD's control, many such Red Army men have risked their lives and escaped to freedom.

SEPTEMBER NINTH rally was Berlin's defiant answer to Stalin. "Today," Mayor Ernst Reuter told the world, "no diplomats and generals address this meeting, but the people of Berlin raise their voices. . . . Peoples of the world . . . give us your help . . . not only by the airlift,

REUTER, Europe's bravest anti-Communist leader, believes peace can be saved by a democratic Russian revolution and urges the West to support the Russian people.

FLOUR for the 2,500,000 blockaded Berliners was unloaded at the Tempelhof airport.

SOCIALISTS sparked Berlin's fight against the Kremlin during the crisis. The banner reads, "Where there is fear, there is no freedom; without freedom, no socialism."

but by standing firmly for our common ideals, which alone can secure both our future and yours." In a radio broadcast a few days earlier, Reuter had said, "If the Russian people could speak out, they would stand here on our side against our common enemy."

"LONG LIVE STALIN, the best friend and helper of Germany" says the banner carried by the Communist "people's police" of East Berlin in a parade celebrating Stalin's birthday. These police receive regular military training under professional soldiers.

SACHSENHAUSEN concentration camp, near Berlin, was taken over by the MVD. Many of the first prisoners were SS men, but Catholic students, trade unionists and Social Democrats soon replaced them. Thousands starved. This photo was snapped secretly in June 1949.

COMMUNAZI police state in East Germany sets up concentration camps, rearms Wehrmacht, regiments youth, cuts living standards, bids for fascist support in the West

Across the street from the Reichstag, on the east side of Brandenburg Gate, the new German police state begins. While West Berliners enjoy freedom, 20,000,-000 other Germans live under a Communist-Nazi despotism headed by Comintern leaders Walter Ulbricht and Wilhelm Pieck. On July 21, 1950, puppet "Prime Minister" Otto Grotewohl told a Party Congress, "The National Front of Democratic Germany does not by any means desire to limit cooperation to democratic forces. On the contrary, we are ready to cooperate with all patriots who have Germany's interests at heart. No patriot who is willing to fight for the justified national interests of the German people will be excluded from the German National Democratic Front." In thus appealing to West German nationalists to rebuild a

CHILDREN in the Soviet occupation zone of Germany learn to salute Stalin's bust.

strong, totalitarian Reich in alliance with the Kremlin, Grotewohl echoed Stalin's pointed message to "President" Pieck in October 1949: "The experience of the last war has shown that the German and Soviet peoples made the largest sacrifices . . . [and] have the largest potentialities in Europe to complete great actions of world significance." Stalin's words were not lost on their intended audience—former SS officers and other anti-democratic elements in West Germany who were embittered by the defeat of Hitler's Reich. The Kremlin's long-range strategy is to make the Soviet zone a nationalistic magnet for the ultimate political conquest of West Germany, with its 45,000,-000 people and its great steel and coal resources. Inasmuch as the Communist Party has only a small following among workers there, the main Soviet-Communist appeal is to military and industrial elements who are cool to the present Bonn government. Stalin hopes to lure them with the prospect of a resurgent Germany linked by profitable trade ties to the Communist states of East Europe and Asia. To this end, the Kremlin is also believed to be financing the neo-fascist "Socialist Reich Party," which advocates West German "neutrality," opposes German participation in European defense, and openly fosters the *Fuehrerprinzip*. In the Soviet zone itself, Communists and

Nazi-militarist elements work together in new paramilitary and security police organizations. The chief of the so-called "people's police" (in reality a cadre army) and of the Communist State Security Service (SSD) is Communist Wilhelm Zaisser, known during the Spanish Civil War as "General Gomez." His deputies include former SS *Obersturmfuehrer* Adelbert Baumler, who runs its political counter-intelligence for West Germany. In charge of radio and press control for the SSD is Dr. Leo Lange, formerly of Himmler's Gestapo. The Moscow League of German Officers administers eleven schools in the Soviet Union to train officers for the "people's police." Among Hitler's former generals who now serve in it are von Lenski, Korfes, Lattmann, Freytag, von Seeckt and Breidthaupt. The brown uniforms of the Hitler Youth have given way to the blue shirts of the Communist Youth, but the Soviet zone shows few other signs that Hitler is gone. Purges follow the usual pattern. From January to June 1951, the Party was engaged in eliminating from its ranks "bandits, saboteurs, arsonists, dynamiters and murderers." Industrial production is at its 1936 level, but the population lives in poverty; meat and dairy products are seldom seen; potatoes are the staple. The new Communist aristocracy, however, easily buys abundance.

WALTER ULBRICHT, the General Secretary of the Soviet zone's Communist Party (which calls itself the "Socialist Unity Party"), is also its brains. "President" Wilhelm Pieck and "Prime Minister" Otto Grotewohl make most of the speeches; Ulbricht plans strategy.

HILDEBRANDT, here interviewing two camera-shy escapees, has said that if the West changes its attitude toward the Stalin regime and "seriously seeks the Russian people's friendship, this will penetrate . . . Russia more quickly than . . . ten new radio transmitters."

F STANDS FOR FREEDOM (*Freiheit*). The revolutionary symbol of the Fighters Against Inhumanity defies the Communist Party from its own headquarters in Beelitz, Soviet zone. Communist courts ruled in May 1951 that the use of this symbol is subversive.

DEMOCRATS fight terror,
lead underground, help Soviet soldiers escape

A militant democratic group in West Berlin, known as the Fighters Against Inhumanity, keeps the spirit of resistance alive in Germany's Soviet zone. Under Rainer Hildebrandt, Ernst Tillich and Guenther Birkenfeld, the Fighters help East Germans and Russian occupation personnel to escape; they broadcast over RIAS (Berlin's free radio) the names of MVD informers; and they smuggle newspapers, pamphlets and books into the Soviet zone. In May 1951, the Fighters joined ex-Soviet officers and Mayor Reuter to form the Freedom Union for German-Russian Friendship, with the aim of developing a resistance front of anti-Stalin elements in the Red Army and the East German citizenry. Men like Hildebrandt live in constant danger of MVD abduction.

INDELIBLE in the hearts of millions behind the Curtain, freedom paints its initial on the cobblestones of an East German town.

CHETNIKS, Serb guerrillas under General Draja Mikhailovich, fought on after the Wehrmacht crushed the Yugoslav regular army (April 6-May 10, 1941). Radio Moscow called Mikhailovich "the patriot leader" in 1942. Chetnik prisoners of the Germans are shown above.

MIKHAILOVICH was captured by Tito's Communist forces on March 25, 1946, tried as a "war criminal" and executed in July. Tito had begun fighting the Germans after Hitler's attack on Russia. Stalin sent him support late in 1942, Great Britain and America in 1943.

YUGOSLAVIA falls to Tito

Josip Broz ("Tito"), a Comintern veteran, was installed as Premier of the coalition government of Yugoslavia on March 6, 1945. The cabinet, approved at Yalta, included two representatives of the Yugoslav Government which had overthrown the pro-Axis regime in 1941 in order to oppose Hitler, but before the year was out, Tito had placed them under house arrest. In November, voters were asked to choose between the Communist "National Front" and the opposition, officially labeled "enemies of the people"; Tito received 90.57 per cent of the vote. He soon abolished press freedom, created a huge secret police (UDBA), per-

TITO'S NEW YUGOSLAV ARMY, BEING EQUIPPED BY AMERICA, IS BIG

PARTISANS under Tito received substantial aid from Britain and the United States; when Tito's headquarters were captured by the Wehrmacht, the British rescued him. The Red Army moved into Yugoslavia in April 1944, and the Partisans captured Belgrade on October 20.

ARCHBISHOP STEPINAC, the Catholic primate of Croatia and Slovenia, was tried as an "enemy of the people" in October 1946 and sentenced to sixteen years in prison. Tito has offered to free Stepinac if he will agree to leave Yugoslavia forever. The prelate has refused.

STALIN and Tito (signing) concluded a "treaty of friendship" in April 1945. Two months later, Tito's Foreign Minister said that Soviet-Yugoslav relations should be based "on the prospect of Yugoslavia becoming in the future a constituent part of the U.S.S.R."

who jails democrats, seizes land, needles Stalin

secuted the clergy, and started forcible collectivization. Supported at first by UNRRA's 2,539,137 tons of supplies, Tito in 1948 began to ask for the industrial goods Stalin had promised; he was also piqued by the Kremlin veto of a Balkan federation. When the Soviets withdrew their missions, Tito complained to Molotov, "We are amazed, we cannot understand, we are deeply hurt." On June 28, 1948, the Cominform expelled Tito's Communists. He then turned to Britain and America and in the next two years received $125,000,000. Although foreign aid has somewhat alleviated Yugoslavia's famine, peasant unrest continues.

ENOUGH TO MAKE HIS SATELLITE NEIGHBORS WARY OF STARTING WAR

"LONG LIVE COMRADE TITO" reads the slogan under this giant poster of Tito in Belgrade. School children carry his portrait and sing, "Comrade Tito, our red rose, our famous country is with you; Comrade Tito, you strawberry in the dew, our people are proud of you."

151

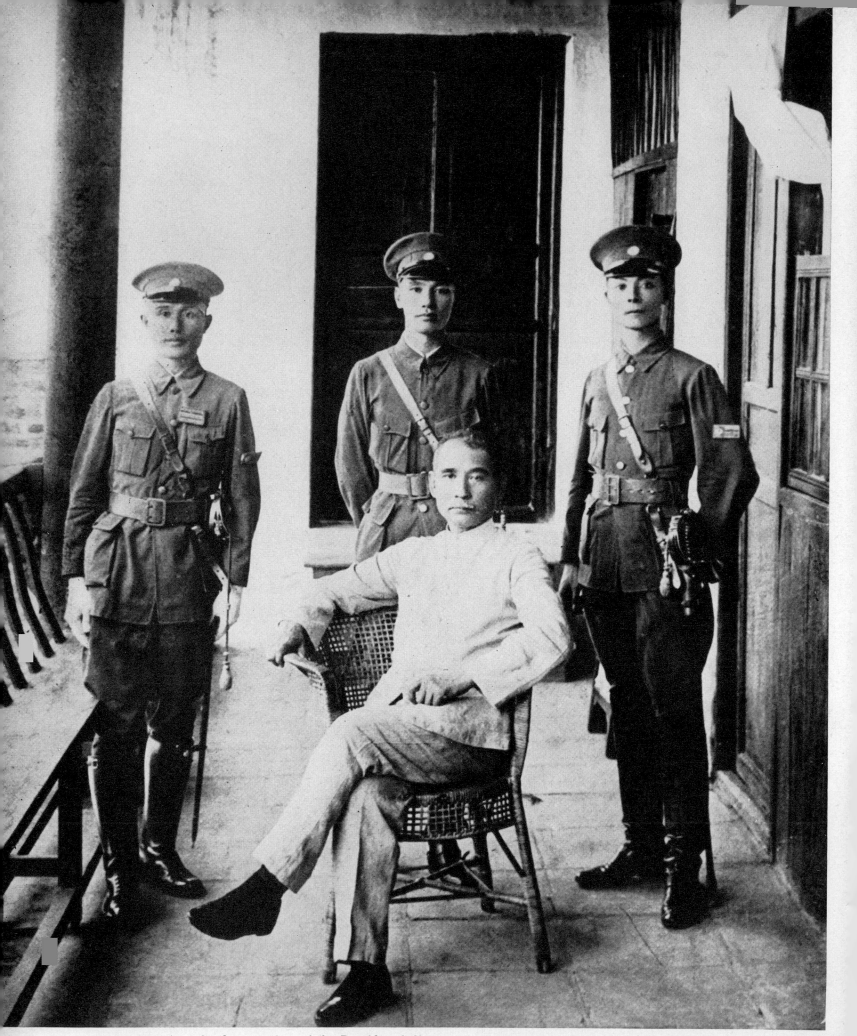

SUN YAT-SEN (seated), first president of the Republic of China, organized the Kuomintang in Canton for the purpose of unifying the nation, and headed it until he died in 1925. He based his program on "Three Principles": national unification, democracy, and social progress. Constitutional democracy, he said, would develop from the county level after a period of Kuomintang tutelage. Sun allowed the Communists to join him, and accepted Soviet aid, but after his death the alliance was dissolved by Chiang Kai-shek (center).

CHINA hungers for peace and national unification, but gets Japanese aggression and civil war with Communists

In 1927, Stalin suffered what appeared to be a crushing defeat in China, when Chiang Kai-shek ended the united front between the National People's Party (Kuomintang) and the Chinese Communist Party. The coalition had been formed in 1924 to unify the country, which regional warlords had ruled since the fall of the Manchus in 1911. Now Chiang broke up the Communist workers' militia, arrested and executed Communist leaders, and forced Soviet advisors to leave. This about-face was a propaganda argument for Trotsky in his last battle against Stalin, who had favored the coalition. In a speech to the Fifteenth Congress of the Party (December 1927), Stalin commented, "The fact that the Chinese revolution has not yet brought a complete victory over imperialism cannot have decisive importance in terms of the perspectives of the revolution. Great popular revolutions never triumph in the first round. They grow and strengthen by ebb and flow. . . . That is how it shall be in China." The "second round" began when the Chinese Communists formed a Soviet government in Kiangsi province, in Central China, under the leadership of Mao Tse-tung, Chou En-lai and Chu Teh. When they were driven from Kiangsi in 1934, they trekked to the remote northwest province of Shensi, made their capital in the village of Yenan and waited for an opportunity to resume their offensive. In 1937, Japanese aggression provided it.

COMMISSAR Michael Borodin organized the combined Kuomintang-Communist armies under Sun Yat-sen. When Chiang dissolved the alliance, Borodin had to leave China.

ATTACKS by Japanese warlords absorbed China's energies for fourteen years. Japanese armies invaded Manchuria in 1931 and Jehol in 1933, paused there, then opened a huge offensive through North and Central China in 1937. By the autumn of 1938, they had captured China's seven largest cities and most of her important industries and railway lines. Although her economy was completely dislocated, China fought on from the new capital of Chungking (above, being bombed by the Japanese) and held off several major onslaughts.

MUKDEN HOTEL displayed pictures of Stalin, Lenin, Sun Yat-sen and Chiang Kai-shek in February 1946, during the collaboration between Stalin and the Central Government. The sign just below the pictures says, "Club for Friendship between China and the Soviet Union."

MANCHURIAN INDUSTRY like the rubber factory above was dismantled by the Soviets. Although Stalin pledged to help the Central Government establish its authority in Manchuria, most of the province was in Communist hands when the Soviet Army departed in March 1946.

FAILURE of U. S. mission to force
coalition government renews China's civil war

Mao Tse-tung promised to cooperate with the Central Government in the war against Japan, but told his Party privately that its policy would be "70 per cent self-development, 20 per cent compromise and 10 per cent fight the Japanese." The Communists inflicted only a tenth of the million casualties which the Japanese suffered in China. At the war's end, the Central Government was in south China, the Japanese held the northern cities, and the Communists the northern countryside; the Soviet Army was occupying Manchuria and soon moved into the ports of Dairen and Port Arthur, which furnish the easiest entry to Manchuria from China. On August 14, 1945, Stalin concluded a thirty-year alliance with the Central Government, and on the 26th, Mao began conferring with Chiang Kai-shek about a coalition. When their parley failed, in October, Government and Communist troops clashed in eleven provinces. The United States sent General Marshall to mediate, at the same time suspending military aid to the Government. He brought about a cease-fire on January 10, 1946, but seven months' talking failed to effect a coalition.

GENERAL MARSHALL visited Yenan during his mission. He is flanked here by Chou En-lai and Chu Teh. Mao Tse-tung is at extreme right.

JAPANESE ARMS helped the Chinese Communists; the Soviets disarmed Japan's crack Kwantung Army (1,100,000 men) and gave its weapons to Mao. The Central Government received some $360,000,000 worth of military equipment from the United States from V-J Day to 1948.

CHINESE GRANDMOTHER SEES HER VILLAGE AFTER IT CHANGED HANDS

CIVIL WAR ravages China;
Japanese arms, Korean troops help Mao win

Although the Communists had used the Marshall "truce" to extend their power from 60 to 300 counties, the government offensive which began in July 1946 drove back Mao's armies and captured Yenan on March 19, 1947. The success of Chiang Kai-shek's forces was only temporary. Over-extended, too fond of walled cities, riddled by corruption, tired of war, they could not match the new Chinese Red Army, reorganized and re-equipped by the Soviets in Manchuria and reinforced by fresh Korean divisions. By the end of the year, the Communists had rolled south of the Yellow River and were marching toward the Yangtse. On Christmas Day, Mao ordered the elimination of "undesirables" from Communist ranks and urged a Cominform for the Far East. Promising an end to war and civil war, division of the land among the peasants, and the defeat of "foreign intervention," Mao's Communists began sweeping all before them in 1948; their path was made easier by autonomous warlords and generals who turned entire armies over to them. When the first sizeable shipment of American arms for the Government left Seattle on November 9, it was too late. Mao entered Peiping on January 22, 1949, and set up his regime there soon afterwards.

COMMUNIST AGITATORS entered Peiping with the Chinese Red Army on January 22, 1949. Here the Political Propaganda Corps distributes pamphlets; elsewhere it staged peasant drum dances. Under Mao, ancient Peiping replaced modern Nanking as capital of China.

DURING THE CIVIL WAR—THE COMMUNISTS CLAIM THEY INFLICTED 8,070,000 CASUALTIES ON CHIANG'S ARMY, ADMITTED 1,600,000 OF THEIR OWN

ON FORMOSA, Chiang Kai-shek reorganized the Central Government's armies (500,000 men) and retrained them, to fend off a Communist invasion. At the same time, he also reorganized the government and army administration, in an effort to eliminate the corruption which had helped bring the Communists to power. General Sun Li-jen, like General Marshall a graduate of Virginia Military Institute, was appointed commander of ground forces. Late in 1950, the U. S. agreed to send Chiang a military mission and more equipment.

MAO TSE-TUNG (left) visited the Kremlin for four months during the 1949-50 winter and signed a formal alliance with Stalin. Between them is Soviet Marshal Bulganin.

TERROR

'People's Control' squads hold mass executions, Hate Weeks

Civil war still rages in China. Today, Mao's Red Army is fighting soldiers, workers and peasants who once welcomed it in the hope that it was bringing peace and a share of the land. Before Mao had ruled a year, almost 2,000,000 guerrillas were battling him from the hills. The West largely ignored China's struggle against Communist despotism, just as it ignored Russia's in 1918-21. It first glimpsed the extent of Mao's terror in June 1951, when his premier, Chou En-lai, announced that the Communists had killed more than a million guerrillas and "saboteurs" in twenty months. Earlier, the Kwantung Military District had revealed the killing of 196,000 "reactionaries" in three provinces during 1950. The Communists launched an indoctrination drive (called "brain-washing") to destroy China's great moral philosophies; they began expunging them from books, plays and films, rewriting history, and staging "Hate Weeks" to whip up frenzy against the non-Communist world. Mao's secret police, the "Commission on People's Control," forced soldiers to collect rice at bayonet-point by threatening them with the execution of their families. (In 1950, almost half the regime's revenue came from this source.) Mass terror reigned in the spring of 1951, with thousands publicly executed in the cities; in one week, 24,000 were arrested in Shanghai. Despite this carnage, the Chinese people are still fighting Mao's dictatorship. After the spring purge, 500,000 ill-equipped guerrillas were still in action.

ON THE FIRST ANNIVERSARY of the Communist regime, October 1, 1950, some 500,000 Pei-ping workers paraded with portraits of Mao. He was then raising a new militia, to supple-

158

ment his Red Army of 5,000,000 and fight anti-Communist guerrillas. Mao once wrote, "A Communist war which lasts ten years may be surprising to other countries, but for us it is only the preface. . . . Historical experience is written in blood and iron."

LAND REFORM enabled 2,000,000 tenant farmers to purchase and till their own land.

COOPERATIVES now have 8,000,000 members in 32,000 villages. Above, a co-op chairman.

JAPAN obtains bill of rights, land reform, equality for women, health program; unions and cooperatives expand

Under American occupation, Japan has experienced broad political and social reforms. The occupation immediately removed all "restrictions on political, civil and religious liberties." Then it ended forced labor, censorship and the secret police; set up independent courts, civil service, and social security laws; and guaranteed equal rights for women. Before the war, only 400,000 workers were organized; now more than 7,000,000 of them belong to Asia's largest labor movement. A public health program has eliminated cholera and sharply reduced tuberculosis, smallpox, diphtheria and typhoid. Under the agrarian law of October 1946, the government bought 27,000,000 plots of land and sold them to tenant farmers, who up to then were tilling 46 per cent of the land. By 1950, the farmers owned and tilled 89 per cent. On January 1, 1950, General MacArthur, under whom these great changes took place, declared, "The myth of the unbridgeable gulf between the ways of the East and the ways of the West has been thoroughly exploded. . . . Men now know that humanity . . . is fundamentally the same in the . . . desire for higher personal dignity, broader individual liberty and a betterment of life." The future of Japan's democracy rests with its people.

KOREA

Communist invasion heightens danger of World War III

The thirty-eighth parallel of latitude cuts Korea almost in half. North of it is a Communist regime, Soviet-sponsored. South of it is the Republic of Korea, founded by the United Nations when North Korea barred them from supervising a free election for the whole country. On June 25, 1950, Communist armies from North Korea, using Soviet tanks and equipment and including divisions seasoned in the Chinese civil war, invaded the Republic. The United States responded at once; President Truman sent American air and naval forces, then infantry divisions from Japan. In the face of Stalin's boycott, the UN approved the U. S. action, and small British, Turkish, French, Philippine and other troops soon moved into the line. The UN forces were cramped into a single beachhead by September, but fought their way out and had liberated almost all of Korea by November, when Mao Tse-tung threw in fresh Chinese armies and drove them back to the Parallel. One year of war cost the Republic of Korea 168,652 military casualties, and the U.S. 73,604; enemy losses were much higher. But the attack shocked the world into realizing the potential disastrousness of not being prepared against Communist aggression.

VISHINSKY and Mao's Wu Hsiu-chuan could not shout the UN into abandoning Korea.

← **KOREAN MEDICS** treat a peasant mother who has been wounded by shell fragments. Roads were jammed by civilians who fled before the advancing Communist troops.

AMERICANS, rushed into the Korean lines to stop the plunging Communists, were unseasoned occupation troops; no other forces were available. General MacArthur had to send all but 5,000 U. S. tro nation of 83,000,000, but veloped. The GI's toughen the grueling combat cond

BALLOT BOXES were brought to the seashore of Numazu Shizuoka so that these fishermen could vote in the 1947 elections, the first in the history of Japan's upper house. The new constitution, passed that same year, outlawed war forever as an instrument of national policy.

EMPEROR HIROHITO renounced his "divine" status in 1946 and soon began going to baseball games, inspecting coal mines, and making frequent public appearances. Before the war, no Japanese could look directly at the "Son of Heaven." Above, Nisei GI's photograph him.

161

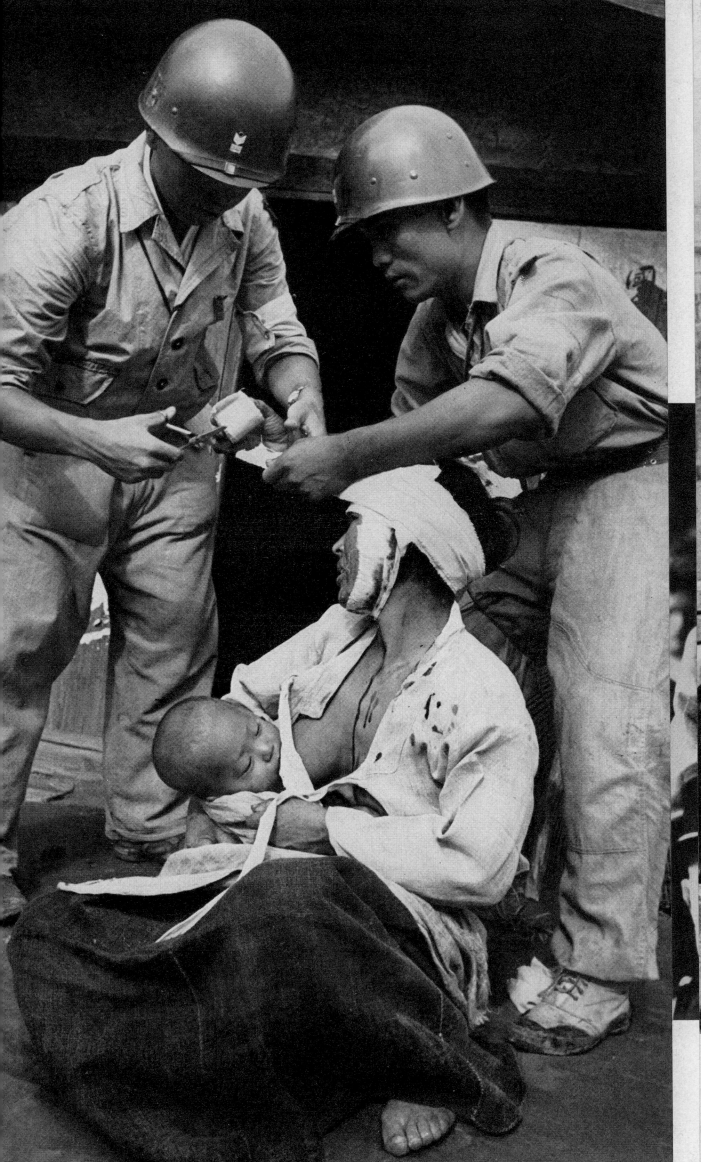

MILITARY TRADITION is bred by sending the sons of army men and the upper bureaucracy to cadet schools. By a decree of August 23, 1943, special entrance facilities were made available to officers' sons. Young cadets undergo stiff training, study tactics and foreign languages. Most instructors are officers who have had combat experience.

EDUCATION has proved a double-edged weapon. The Party finds that the official doctrines hammered into student minds have caused strong "apolitical" reactions. On the other

THE COLLECTIVE FARMERS

More than two decades have passed since Stalin ordered the "liquidation of the kulaks as a class," in order to destroy the independent farmers as an anti-Communist force and to obtain greater grain reserves for the purchase of heavy machinery abroad. Despite the vast human cost of forcible collectivization, neither objective has yet been realized. During the last three years before World War II, Russia was producing less grain than in 1928, and three years after the war she was producing less than under Tsarism —only 850 pounds per capita as compared to 1,033 in 1909-13. The political

failure has been even more marked. Stalin had installed trained Communists to run the collective farm communities. (On January 11, 1933, the Central Committee of the Communist Party ordered that 17,000 "picked and seasoned Bolsheviks" be sent to man the collectives and the tractor stations.) Within a few years, however, they had begun to support the local interests of the farmers and had helped them acquire "illegal" private plots. After the war, Moscow discovered that thousands of collectives had been broken up with the active assistance of the Party-trained overseers. In 1946, the Council of Ministers and the Party Central Committee condemned this grass-roots revolt against the collectives, but the practice went on. In 1950, Stalin started an ambitious new scheme to subjugate the farmers—they were to be moved out of their villages and settled in large "agricultural cities," still to be built. The program, pushed hard at first, was suspended a few months later because of farmers' widespread resistance.

THE NEW GENERATION

The outlook of the new generation, particularly the sons and daughters of the ruling class who can afford higher education, is a matter of serious concern to the Kremlin. A Russian-speaking American observer, Professor Barghoorn, who was in the U.S.S.R. in 1942-47, has described their attitude as "a sort of Soviet anti-clericalism"—acute skepticism to-

ward Party dogma. The glaring contrast between the Party's words and deeds, the moral gulf dividing Stalinist doctrine from the Russian classics studied in schools, are germinating seeds of inner revolt beyond the Politburo's control.

THE PARTY AND SECRET POLICE

The present regime's power over Russia rests on the Party and the secret police. In the early Lenin days, the ranks of both were filled by fanatics who sincerely believed—as many non-Russian Communists still believe—that a better society could be constructed by means of terror. Such men are hard to find in the Soviet

PIROGOV, Soviet airman, escaped in 1948 by flying from the Ukraine to the U. S. zone of Austria—one of thousands of Russian veterans who risk their lives to become free.

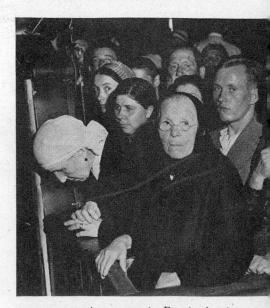

RELIGION remains strong in Russia despite the Party's thirty years' war against it. In the last war, churches were packed with front-bound troops. In 1948, Party members

hand, the works of Pushkin, Tolstoy, Chekhov are avidly read by far more young Russians than ever before, indicating a search for new values. Above, Moscow University.

RED SQUARE TANKS display the armed power of Russia. To pay for the huge army and war industry, the people continue to live on short rations. In the basic sinews of war,

Russia still lags far behind America (less than one-seventh of the oil, less than a third of the steel, and a little more than one-third of the coal output of the U. S.)

Communist Party and the MVD today. Life has demonstrated to them the truth of Alexander Herzen's prophecy in 1867 that socialism without liberty "would soon degenerate into autocratic communism." In the Party and the police, the degeneration began while Lenin was alive, proceeded quickly during the great purges, and has been completed since. The selfless fanatics perished long ago; by 1939, about 70 per cent of the Party was filled with men and women who had joined after 1928. Today, Party membership is the bureaucratic price for obtaining good jobs; the secret police has become the palace guard of a hated oligarchy. The doctrines that are still hammered home with deadening monotony find little acceptance in their minds, because life outside the Kremlin palace and the fashionable resorts of the ruling caste has made a mockery of Lenin's promised "classless society." Privilege and fear are the chains that still bind Party and MVD members of the oligarchy. The better elements, whom the Party still recruits for their brains and energy, continue to serve Stalin chiefly because they see no safe way to replace the present regime. Those who are capable of self-sacrifice for freedom—and their number is legion—are also held together by the fear, insidiously nurtured by the Kremlin and reinforced by some actions of the West, that any radical internal change would provide foreign enemies with an opportunity to pounce on Russia. To banish that fear from the minds of those Party members and police troops who detest the regime and can do so much to destroy it, is one of the challenges that Russia offers to the statesmanship of the western world.

obstacle to the return of peace and freedom in Russia, they become the potential soldiers of democratic revolution. No man is more sensitive to this situation than is Joseph Stalin. Every western gesture that implies hostility to the Russian people, rather than to Communist tyranny, is exploited by his gigantic propaganda machine in an effort to convince the army that in the long run his despotism, for all its cruelties, is a less permanent threat to Russia's survival than is foreign aggression. World peace may therefore depend on the West's capacity to place the democratic alternative to a new world war within the grasp of the officers and soldiers of the Soviet Army.

THE SOVIET ARMY

The officers and soldiers of the Soviet Army are the most important imponderable force in the world today. Fighting for the preservation of their country, they were strong enough in 1942-45 to wreck Europe's most formidable army. Unwilling to fight, they constitute an impassable barrier on the road to a third world war. If western deeds arouse them to the realization that Stalin's regime is the sole

who "hindered" anti-religious propaganda were threatened with expulsion. Parents who continued to give religious instruction to their children were also warned to desist.

MOSLEMS like this camel driver of Bokhara have fought tenaciously to defend their faith against Communist attack. The Party wages open war against all denominations.

169

ELINOR LIPPER, born in Holland, went to Moscow in 1937 and was arrested a few months later. She spent eleven years in slave camps, mainly in notorious Magadan, which Vice President Wallace visited in 1944 and described admiringly in his book, *Soviet Asia Mission*.

ANATOL ZURICHENKO (left), arrested after the death of Politburo member Kirov in 1935, was sent to the North Russian camps where, he recalls, "We dragged logs out of the river with our bare hands. At night, after a morsel of bread and thin soup . . . we were driven into filthy barracks to sleep on lice-ridden plank beds." Constantin Sibirsky (right), former Soviet movie-script writer, served four years in Siberia for possessing a copy of John Reed's *Ten Days That Shook the World*. He is now employed by a Brooklyn real estate firm.

LUDWIG GOLUBOVICH (left), a former NKVD inspector in the Bamlag camps of Northern Siberia, later spent five years there as a prisoner. In May 1951, he testified at public hearings on Soviet slave labor, conducted in Brussels by a group of former Nazi concentration camp inmates headed by David Rousset (right), French Socialist writer. Eight months before, in Paris, Rousset had won a spectacular libel suit against the Communist paper *Les Lettres Françaises*, which accused him of having invented his facts on slave labor.

SLAVE LABOR

Stalin's biggest enterprise is the final product of a system which has reached a dead end

Under Tsar Nicholas II, Russia's most hated institution was penal servitude, which, according to the *Small Soviet Encyclopedia*, reached its peak in 1913 with 32,757 prisoners, some 5000 of whom were revolutionists, the rest criminals. Under Stalin, estimates of the slave labor population run from 10,000,000 to 15,000,000. Soviet concentration camps started in 1918. "I don't know how Lenin and Trotsky feel about this proceeding," Thomas Mann wrote in 1925, "but I am sure that Karl Marx would turn in his grave." In 1930, the planning commissions were instructed "to incorporate the work performed by those deprived of liberty into the planned economy of the Five Year Plan." The GPU accordingly established the Main Administration for Corrective Labor Camps (GULAG). It soon became the greatest slave enterprise in history, as millions of farmers were deported to Arctic lumber areas and Siberian mines. In certain parts of Siberia, the GULAG chiefs became governors of slave provinces larger than many European countries. By 1937, there were 5,000,000 to 6,000,000 inmates in camps in North Russia, Central Asia and Northern Siberia. In 1941, the NKVD was assigned 14 per cent of the state budget for capital construction, the largest share going to GULAG. Stalin's occupation of Eastern Poland and the Baltic states added millions of new victims. Poles who were later freed under the Soviet-Polish treaty of July 1941 have furnished a large part of the documentation on Soviet slave labor, like the NKVD documents at the right. During and after the war, nationalities suspected of disloyalty to the regime—Volga Germans, Crimean Tartars, etc.—were deported en masse. On August 1, 1951, *Pravda* claimed that the camps existed only for "enemies of the people . . . landlords and capitalists . . . incorrigible thieves . . . subversive agents . . . terrorists and assassins sent in by foreign secret services," all of whom are "out to restore capitalism in the U.S.S.R., to restore the exploitation of man by man, to drench the country in the blood of the workers and farmers." *Pravda* did not say how many millions have died in these camps in the past twenty years.

MAGADAN
In Khabarovsk region

SEVURALLAG
In Sverdlovsk region

KOTLAS
In Archangel region

VORKUTSTROY
In Vorkuta region

LAVRENTI P. BERIA, of the Politburo, is chief of police and punitive agencies, supervisor of slave labor, and atomic energy. Stalin introduced him to Ribbentrop as "the head of my Gestapo."

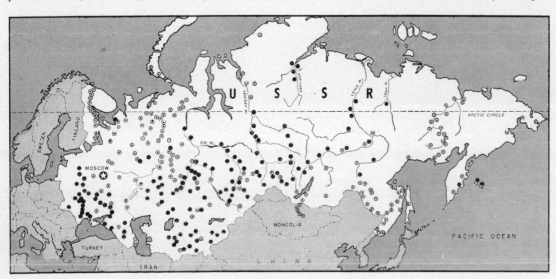

EACH DOT on the map stands for a slave labor camp. The sites were pinpointed by 14,000 affidavits collected by the American Federation of Labor from former inmates who escaped or were released.

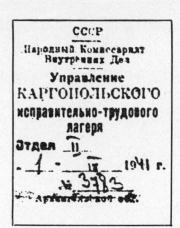

KARGOPOL
In Archangel region

KARAGANDA
In Karaganda region

USOL
In Solikamsk region

KANSK
In Krasnoyarsk region

INDEX

INDEX

BIBLIOGRAPHY

Alliluyeva, A. S., Stalin's Sister-in-law, *Reminiscences*. Moscow, 1946. The Soviet Writer (in Russian).

Alpert, Paul. *Twentieth Century Economic History of Europe*. Henry Schuman. New York, 1951.

Armstrong, Hamilton Fish. *Tito and Goliath*. The Macmillan Company. New York, 1951.

Barghoorn, Frederick C. *The Soviet Image of the United States*. Harcourt, Brace and Company. New York, 1950.
"The Soviet Union Between War and Cold War." *The Annals of the American Academy of Political and Social Science*. May, 1949.

Barre, Suda Lorena and Lutz, Ralph Haswell. *Organization of American Relief in Europe 1918-1919*. Stanford University Press. Stanford University, California, 1943.

Bibineishvili, B. *Kamo*. Old Bolshevik Publishing House. Moscow, 1934. In Russian.

Blueprint for World Conquest. As Outlined by the Communist International. Human Events. Washington and Chicago, 1946.

Blythe, Henry. *Spain Over Britain*. George Routledge, London, 1937.

Borkenau, Franz. *The Communist International*. Faber and Faber. London, 1938.
The Spanish Cockpit. Faber and Faber. London, 1937.

Bornstein, Joseph. *The Politics of Murder*. William Sloane Associates. New York, 1950.

Brenner, Anita. *Class War in Spain*. The Socialist Labor Party of Australia. Sydney, 1937.

Buckley, Henry. *The Life and Death of the Spanish Republic*. Hamish Hamilton. London, 1940.

Bunyan, James and Fisher, H. H. *The Bolshevik Revolution 1917-1918*. Hoover War Library Publication No. 3. Stanford University Press. Stanford University, California, 1934.

Byrnes, James F. *Speaking Frankly*. Harper & Brothers. New York, 1947.

Carman, E. Day. *Soviet Imperialism*. Public Affairs Press. Washington, D.C., 1950.

Chamberlin, William Henry. *The Russian Revolution 1917-1921*. The Macmillan Company, 1935.

Chernov, Victor. *The Birth of Revolutionary Russia*. Paris-Prague-New York, 1934. In Russian.

Churchill, Winston S. *Speech at the British-Russian Club in London, July, 21, 1919*.
The Gathering Storm. Houghton Mifflin Company. Boston, 1948.
Their Finest Hour. Houghton Mifflin Company. Boston, 1949.
The Grand Alliance. Houghton Mifflin Company. Boston, 1950.
The Hinge of Fate. Houghton Mifflin Company. Boston, 1950.

Clay, Lucius D. *Decision in Germany*. Doubleday and Company. New York, 1950.

Counts, George S. and Lodge, Nucia. *The Country of the Blind*. Houghton Mifflin Company. Boston, 1949.

Crankshaw, Edward. *Cracks in the Kremlin Wall*. The Viking Press. New York, 1951.

Dallin, David J. *The Real Soviet Russia*. Yale University Press. New Haven, 1947.

Dallin, David J. and Nicolaevsky, Boris I. *Forced Labor in Soviet Russia*. Yale University Press. New Haven, 1947.

Deane, John R. *The Strange Alliance*. The Viking Press. New York, 1946.

Deutscher, Isaac. *Stalin, A Political Biography*. Oxford University Press. New York and London, 1949.

Documents on the Mindszenty Case. Budapest. 1949.

Eisenhower, Dwight D. *Crusade in Europe*. Doubleday and Company. New York, 1948.

Fearey, Robert A. *The Occupation of Japan, Second Phase: 1948-1950*. Published under the auspices of the International Secretariat, Institute of Pacific Relations. The Macmillan Company. New York, 1950.

Figner, Vera. *Memoirs of a Revolutionist*. International Publishers. New York, 1927.

Fischer, Louis (ed.). *Thirteen Who Fled*. Harper and Brothers. New York, 1949.

Fischer, Ruth. *Stalin and German Communism*. Harvard University Press. Cambridge, 1948.

Foltz, Charles Jr. *The Masquerade in Spain*. Houghton Mifflin Company. Boston, 1948.

Freedom Through Friendship. Published by the Freedom Union for German-Russian Friendship. Addresses by Ernst Reuter, Guenther Birkenfeld, Rainer Hildebrandt, Gregory Klimov, Eugene Romanov, Alexander Trushnovitch. Berlin, 1951. In German.

Gankin, Olga Hess and Fisher, H. H. *The Bolsheviks and the World War*. The Hoover Library on War, Revolution and Peace Publication No. 15. Stanford University Press. Stanford University, California, 1940.

Gitlow, Benjamin. *The Whole of Their Lives*. Charles Scribner's Sons. New York and London, 1948.

Gliksman, Jerzy. *Tell The West*. Gresham Press. New York, 1948.

Goebbels, Joseph. *The Goebbels Diaries*. Edited and Translated by Louis P. Lochner. Doubleday and Company. New York, 1948.

Gordon, Manya. *Workers Before and After Lenin*. E. P. Dutton and Company, Inc. New York, 1941.

Gsovski, Vladimir. *Soviet Civil Law*. University of Michigan Law School. Ann Arbor, 1948.
"Elements of Soviet Labor Law." *The Monthly Labor Review*, March, 1951.

Gunther, John. *The Riddle of MacArthur*. Harper and Brothers. New York, 1950.

History of the All-Union Communist Party (Bolsheviks)—Short Course. State Publishing House of Political Literature. Moscow, 1938. In Russian.

Historicus. "Stalin on Revolution," *Foreign Affairs*, January, 1949.

Hitler, Adolf. *Mein Kampf*. Reynal and Hitchcock. New York, 1940.
My New Order. Reynal and Hitchcock. New York, 1941.

Howley, Frank. *Berlin Command*. G. B. Putnam's Sons. New York, 1950.

Hunter, Edward. "Red China's Hate Week." *The New Leader*, September 30, 1950.
"Brain-Washing in New China." *The New Leader*, October 20, 1950.

In Memory Of Those Who Perished. Edited by N. I. Astrov, V. F. Zeeler, P. N. Miliukov, V. A. Obolensky, S. A. Smirnov and L. E. Elyashchev. Societe Nouvelle d'Editions Franco-Slaves. Paris, 1929. In Russian.

Iremashvili, Joseph. *Stalin and the Tragedy of Georgia*. Berlin, 1931. In German.

Ivanovich, Stephen. *The Red Army*. Contemporary Notes. Paris, 1931. In Russian.

Jelagin, Juri. *Taming of the Arts*. E. P. Dutton and Company. New York, 1951.

Karpovich, Michael. *Imperial Russia, 1801-1917*. Henry Holt and Company. New York, 1932.

Kasenkina, Oksana. *Leap to Freedom*. J. B. Lippincott Company. Philadelphia and New York, 1949.

Kennan, George F. "America and the Russian Future." *Foreign Affairs*, April, 1951.

Khachapuridze, G. V. *The Bolsheviks of Georgia in the Struggle for the Triumph of Soviet Power*. Gosizdat. Moscow, 1947. In Russian.

Kintner, William R. *The Front Is Everywhere*. Militant Communism in Action. University of Oklahoma Press. Norman, Oklahoma, 1950.

Koestler, Arthur. *The Yogi and the Commissar*. The Macmillan Company. New York, 1945.

Reports, Collected or Edited Volumes

BIBLIOGRAPHY

Kogon, Eugen. *The SS State*. Tempelhof Publishing House. Berlin, 1947. In German.

Kotschnig, Walter. "Forced Labor." *Vital Speeches of the Day*, April 1, 1951.

Kravchenko, Victor. *I Chose Justice*. Charles Scribner's Sons. New York, 1950.

Krivitsky, W. G. *In Stalin's Secret Service*. Harper & Brothers. New York, 1939.

Labin, Suzanne. *Stalin's Russia*. Victor Gollancz Ltd., London, 1949.

Laserson, Max M. *The American Impact On Russia*. 1784-1917. Macmillan, New York, 1950.

Lasky, Melvin J. "Inside Soviet Germany." *The New Leader*, April 16-May 7, 1951.

Lasky, Victor. "We Were Soviet Slaves." *Pageant*, March, 1951.

Latsis, M. Y. *Two Years of Struggle on the Internal Front*. State Publishing House. Moscow, 1920. (In Russian.)

Lehrman, Hal. *Russia's Europe*. D. Appleton-Century Company. New York, 1947.
Letter of An Old Bolshevik. The Key to the Moscow Trials. Rand School Press. New York, 1937.

Lipper, Elinor. *Eleven Years in Soviet Prison Camps*. Henry Regnery. Chicago, 1951.

Lyons, Eugene. *Assignment in Utopia*. Harcourt, Brace and Company. New York, 1937.
The Red Decade. The Bobbs-Merrill Company. New York, 1941.
Stalin. J. B. Lippincott Company. Philadelphia, 1940.
Letters From Russian Prisons. Consisting of reprints of documents by political prisoners in Soviet prisons, prison camps and exile, and reprints of affidavits concerning political persecution in Soviet Russia, official statements by Soviet authorities, excerpts from Soviet laws pertaining to civil liberties, and other documents. Albert and Charles Boni. New York, 1925.

Madariaga, Salvador de. *Spain*. Jonathan Cape. London and Toronto, 1942.

Martin, David. *Ally Betrayed*. Prentice-Hall. New York, 1946.

Martin, Edwin M. *The Allied Occupation of Japan*. Published under the auspices of the Institute of Pacific Relations. Stanford University Press. Stanford University, California, 1948.

Mendizabal, Alfredo. *The International Implications of the Spanish Problem*. The New Leader. New York, 1947.

Mikolajczyk, Stanislaw. *The Rape of Poland*. Whittlesey House. New York, 1948.

Miliukov, Paul. *Outlines of Russian Culture* (edited by Michael Karpovich). University of Pennsylvania Press. Philadelphia, 1942.
Russia Today and Tomorrow. The Macmillan Company. New York, 1922.

Mitchell, Broadus. *Depression Decade*. Rinehart. New York, 1947.

Mora, Silvester. *Kolyma, Gold and Forced Labor in the USSR*. Foundation for Foreign Affairs. Washington, 1949.

Morrow, Felix. *Revolution and Counter-Revolution in Spain*. Pioneer Publishers. New York, 1938.

Nagy, Ferenc. *The Struggle Behind the Iron Curtain*. The Macmillan Company. New York, 1948.
Nazi Conspiracy and Aggression. Volume III. International Military Trials. Nurnberg, 1946.
Nazi-Soviet Relations, 1939-1941. Documents from the Archives of the German Foreign Office. United States Department of State. Washington, 1948.

Nichols, William I. "Needed Now: An Emancipation Proclamation for the Russian People." *This Week Magazine*, October 1, 1950.

Nicolaevsky, Boris I. "Stalin's New War on the Peasants." *The New Leader*, January 1, 1951.
"The Split on Soviet Farm Policy." *The New Leader*, May 21, 1951.
Not Guilty. Report of the Commission of Inquiry into the Charges Made against Leon Trotsky in the Moscow Trials. Harper and Brothers. New York, 1938.

Orwell, George. *Homage to Catalonia*. Sacker and Warburg. London, 1938.

Pares, Bernard. *Russia*. Penguin Books. Harmondsworth. Middlesex, 1940.

Pirogov, Peter. *Why I Escaped*. Duell, Sloan and Pearce. New York, 1950.

Plekhanov, George. *A Year in the Motherland*. J. Povolozky and Company. Paris, 1921. In Russian.

Radkey, Oliver Henry. *The Election to the Russian Constituent Assembly of 1917*. Harvard Historical Monograph Number XXI. Harvard University Press. Cambridge, 1950.

Reed, John. *Ten Days That Shook the World*. The Modern Library, New York, 1935.
Report on the Communist "Peace" Offensive. Committee on Un-American Activities, House of Representatives. Washington, 1951.

Rossi, A. *A Communist Party in Action*. Yale University Press. New Haven, 1949.
Two Years of German-Soviet Alliance. Arthème Fayard. Paris, 1949. In French.

Sack, A. J. *The Birth of Russian Democracy*. Russian Information Bureau. New York, 1918.

Scott, John. *Behind the Urals*. Houghton Mifflin Company. Boston, 1942.

Shachtman, Max. "Is Russia A Socialist Community?" *The New International*, May-June, 1950.

Shaplen, Robert. "Guerrillas—Our Hope in Red China." *Collier's*, July 21, 1951.

Sharp, Samuel L. *New Constitutions in the Soviet Sphere*. Foundation for Foreign Affairs, Washington, D.C., 1950.

Sherwood, Robert E. *Roosevelt and Hopkins*. Harper and Brothers. New York, 1948.

Shub, Boris. *The Choice*. Duell, Sloan and Pearce. New York, 1950.

Shub, David. *Lenin: A Biography*. Doubleday and Company, Inc. New York, 1948.

Slonim, Marc. *The Epic of Russian Literature from Its Origins Through Tolstoy*. Oxford University Press. New York, 1950.

Souvarine, Boris. *Stalin*. A Critical Survey of Bolshevism. Longmans, Green and Co., New York, 1939.

Stalin, J. V. *Collected Works, Volumes 1-13*. Ogiz. State Publishing House of Political Literature. Moscow, 1946-1951. In Russian.
Problems of Leninism. Foreign Languages Publishing House. Moscow, 1940.
On the Great Patriotic War of the Soviet Union. Ogiz. State Publishing House of Political Literature. Moscow, 1946. In Russian.

Stanford, Neal. "How The Communists Captured Czechoslovakia." *American Mercury*, September, 1949.

Steinberg, Julien (ed.). *Verdict of Three Decades*. Duell, Sloan and Pearce. New York, 1950.

Stettinius, Edward R., Jr. *Lend-Lease, Weapon for Victory*. The Macmillan Company. New York, 1944.

Stevens, Edmund. *This Is Russia—Uncensored*. Didier. New York, 1950.

Stewart, George. *The White Armies of Russia*. The Macmillan Company. New York, 1933.

Stypulkowski, Z. *Invitation to Moscow*. Thames and Hudson. London, 1951.
Tensions Within The Soviet Union. Prepared by the Legislative Reference Service of the Library of Congress, for the use of the Senate Committee on Foreign Relations. Washington, 1951.
The Case of Henryk Erlich and Victor Alter. General Jewish Workers' Union of Poland. London, 1943.

Swift, Stephen K. *The Cardinal's Story*—The Life and Work of Joseph Cardinal Mindszenty. The Macmillan Company. New York, 1949.

The Case of Leon Trotsky. Report of Hearings on the Charges Made against Him in the Moscow Trials by the Preliminary Commission of Inquiry. Harper & Brothers. New York, 1937.

The Case of the Trotskyite-Zinovievite Terrorist Centre. Report of Court Proceedings Heard Before the Military Collegium of the Supreme Court of the U.S.S.R. People's Commissariat of Justice of the U.S.S.R., Moscow, 1936.

The Case of the Anti-Soviet Trotskyite Centre. Report of Court Proceedings Heard before the Military Collegium of the Supreme Court of the U.S.S.R. People's Commissariat of Justice of the U.S.S.R., Moscow, 1937.

The Case of the Anti-Soviet "Bloc of Rights and Trotskyites." Report of Court Proceedings Heard before the Military Collegium of the Supreme Court of the U.S.S.R. People's Commissariat of Justice of the U.S.S.R., Moscow, 1938.

The Laval Trial. Collection of Great Contemporary Trials. Editions Albin Michael. Paris, 1946. In French.

The Strategy and Tactics of World Communism. Supplement III. C. Communism in China. Committee on Foreign Affairs, House of Representatives. Washington, 1948.

The Truth About Kronstadt. A collection of documents, including the *Izvestia of the Revolutionary Committee of the Sailors, Red Army Men and Workers of Kronstadt*, Prague, 1921. (In Russian.)

The Twelve Who Are To Die. The Trial of the Socialist Revolutionaries. Published by the Delegation of the Party of the Socialist Revolutionists. Berlin, 1922.

Trotsky, Leon. *Stalin, An Appraisal of the Man and his Influence*. Harper & Brothers Publishers. New York and London, 1941.
Problems of the Chinese Revolution. Pioneer Publishers. New York, 1932.

United States Relations With China. United States Department of State. Washington, 1949.

UNRRA, Report of Director General to the Council for the period 1 July 1947 to 31 December 1947 and Summary of Operations 9 November 1943 to 31 December 1947. Washington, 1948.

Utley, Freda. *The China Story*. Henry Regnery Company. Chicago, 1951.

Wallace, Henry A. *Soviet Asia Mission*. Reynal and Hitchcock. New York, 1946.

Walling, William English. *Russia's Message*. Doubleday-Page & Co., New York, 1908.

Walsh, Edmund, A. *The Fall of the Russian Empire*. Blue Ribbon Books, Inc. New York, 1927.

Wasson, R. Gordon. *Towards A Russian Policy*. A Second Look at Some Popular Beliefs About Russia and the Soviet Regime. Overbrook Press. Stamford, Conn., 1951.

Wheeler-Bennett, John W. *Munich: Prologue to Tragedy*. Duell, Sloan and Pearce. New York, 1948.

White, Leigh. *Balkan Caesar*. Charles Scribner's Sons. New York, 1951.

Wolfe, Bertram D. *Three Who Made a Revolution*. The Dial Press. New York, 1948.

Wood, William A. (with Sieve, Myriam). *Our Ally: The People of Russia*. Charles Scribner's Sons. New York, 1950.

Yershov, Vasily. "I Saw Slavery in Russia's Cities." *The New Leader*, April 9, 1951.

Yourievsky, E. "What the Figures Tell Us." *Narodnaya Pravda*, Paris, April, 1951. In Russian.

Ypsilon. *Pattern for World Revolution*. Ziff-Davis Publishing Company. Chicago, 1947.

Zenzinov, Vladimir. *Meeting With Russia*. Letters to the Red Army. New York, 1945. In Russian.

PICTURE CREDITS

The following list by pages shows the source from which each picture was obtained. Where several sources appear on one page, pictures from left to right are separated by commas; from top to bottom, by dashes; unless otherwise indicated. Wherever pictures are not credited, sources prefer anonymity.

Book Jacket: Sovfoto

6, 7: Pictures Inc., LIFE *photo by* Walter Sanders, LIFE *photo by* Alfred Eisenstaedt

8, 9: Sovfoto

10, 11: *lt.* Alexander B. Willis *exc. bot.* LIFE *photo by* Margaret Bourke-White; *cen. from* "Stalin, An Appraisal of The Man And His Influence" *by* Leon Trotsky *pub. by* Harper Bros., *courtesy* N.Y. Public Library

13: Historical Pictures Service— Brown Bros.

14: *from* "Dance Memoranda" *by* Merle Armitage *pub. by* Duell, Sloan & Pearce

15: *t. from* "Birth of Russian Democracy" Sovfoto (2)— *bot. lt. from* "Birth of Russian Democracy" *by* Arcady Joseph Sack, *rt.* Culver

17: *t. rt. from* "Birth of Russian Democracy" (2)

18, 19: *lt.* Underwood & Underwood— Keystone View Co.; *rt.* James Hare

20, 21: *t. lt. & rt.* Historical Pictures Service— *cen. rt. from* "Three Who Made a Revolution" *by* Bertram Wolfe *pub. by* Dial Press, Inc.— *bot. rt.* Historical Pictures Service

23: *rt. from* "Three Who Made a Revolution"

26, 27: Int., Historical Pictures Service; *rt. cen. from* "Stalin, An Appraisal of the Man and His Influence" *by* Leon Trotsky

28, 29: *lt. cen. from* "Birth of Russian Democracy" *bot. lt.* Historical Pictures Service, *bot. 2nd from rt.* Sovfoto

30, 31: *t. lt.* W.W., Keystone View Co.

33: *t. rt.* European Picture Service— *bot. lt.* Keystone View Co.

PICTURE CREDITS

36: Monkemeyer Press—*from* "The White Armies of Russia" *by* George Stewart *pub. by* The MacMillan Co.
38: *bot. rt.* W.W.
39: W.W.
40: Int.—Historical Pictures Service (2)
41: Underwood & Underwood
42, 43: *t. cen.* Acme, Int.—*bot. 2nd from rt.* Keystone View Co.
44: *bot. lt.* Int.
46: *t. lt.* Sovfoto
47: Keystone View Co.
48, 49: Acme, Int.—*lt.* Max Pohly *from* B.S., European Picture Service
51: *lt.* Int.; *rt.* Int.—*from* "Stalin, a New World Seen Through One Man" *by* Henri Barbusse *pub. by* The MacMillan Co.
53: *t.* W.W.
54, 55: *t. lt.* W.W. (2)
56, 57: *t. lt.* W.W.; *bot. rt.* Sovfoto
58: Int., W.W.—Acme, St. Louis Star-Times
59: W.W.—Acme
60: *t. rt.* Historical Pictures Service—W.W.
61: Underwood & Underwood
62, 63: *lt.* Max Pohly *from* B.S.—Int.—Max Pohly *from* B.S.; *cen.* Pictures Inc.; *bot. rt.* Acme
65: W.W.—Int.
66, 67: W.W., Int.,—Chim, LIFE *photo by* Larry Burrows, B.S., W.W., Jack Allen Grau
68, 69: Int. (3), Sovfoto; *rt.* LIFE *photo by* Margaret Bourke-White, PIX—*bot. rt.* W.W.
70: Sovfoto—Int.—Int.
72: Int., Acme—LIFE *photo by* Francis Miller
73: Int., W.W. (2) Int.
74: *cen. rt.* Sovfoto
77: *bot.* W.W.
78: *lt.* W.W.—Int. (3)
79: W.W.
80: W.W.—Combine
82: W.W.
83: *lt.* Int.; *rt.* News of the Day Newsreel *from* Int.—Acme—W.W. (2)
84, 85: *lt.* W.W.; *rt.* Int.—News of the Day Newsreel *from* Int.—Acme
86: Int.—Int., Holbech & Gulbransen *from* B.S.
87: W.W., LIFE *photo by* Carl Mydans—W.W., LIFE *photo by* Carl Mydans
88: Cinematrographique de l'Armee
89: Dever *from* B.S.—Acme—*lt.* W.W.
90: LIFE *photo by* George Rodger
91: European Picture Service—British Official *photo*

92: *t.* U.S. Army *photos*
93: U.S. Army *photo,* Acme—W.W.
94: Dever *from* B.S.—British Official *photo,* Acme
95: Pictures Inc.
96: *t.* W.W.
98: British Official *photos*
99: *bot.* Sovfoto, W.W.
100: W.W.
101: *rt.* Sovfoto (2)—LIFE *photo by* Margaret Bourke-White
102, 103: *t. lt.* U.S. Signal Corps *photo; rt.* LIFE *photo by* Alfred Eisenstaedt—LIFE *photo by* Frank Scherschel
104, 105: *bot. lt.* Int. (2), U.S. Army Signal Corps *photo; rt.* Acme—Int.
106: LIFE *photo by* Robert Capa—U.S. Signal Corps *photo*—Rene Zuber
107: LIFE *photo by* Ralph Morse—Acme (2), W.W.
108, 109: *lt.* U.S. Signal Corps *photo*—Int.; *rt.* W.W.—Int.
110, 111: Sovfoto *exc. bot. rt.*
112: LIFE *photo by* Johnny Florea—LIFE *photo by* Gronefeld
113: LIFE *photo by* Margaret Bourke-White
114: USAAF *photo*
115: *lt.* Chinese News Service, *from* Acme—LIFE *photo by* Johnny Florea; Int.
116, 117: U.S. Navy *photo,* LIFE *photo by* George Silk—Int.
118, 119: *t. lt. courtesy* Jewish Socialist Bund (3)
121: *t.* Sovfoto
122: W.W.
123: Acme—*courtesy* American Red Cross
124: W.W. (2)—Acme—Int., Acme
125: W.W.
126, 127: *lt.* W.W.—European Picture Service—Wilfred Burchett; *cen.* Werner Bischof *from* Magnum; *rt.* W.W.—Keystone
128, 129: *t.* Acme *exc. lt.; cen.* Harris & Ewing, Sovfoto; *bot. cen.* U.S. Official *photo from* OWI, Acme
130, 131: W.W. *exc. rt.* Topical Press
132: Acme
133: W.W.
134, 135: *lt.* Int.; *cen.* B.S.—*rt.* Tibor Bass—LIFE *photo by* John Phillips, Hungarian Bulletin Photo Service—W.W.
136: British Official *photo,* W.W., Acme—David Seymour *from* Magnum—W.W., LIFE *photo by* Dmitri Kessel
137: W.W.
138: LIFE *photo by* N.R. Farbman—W.W., Keystone
139: PIX, Int., LIFE *photo by*

N. R. Farbman—*courtesy* Paix et Liberte, W.W.
140: David Seymour *from* Magnum
141: *t.* Reg Ingraham; *bot. rt.* LIFE *photos by* Dmitri Kessel (2)
142, 143: *lt.* Sovfoto—LIFE *photo by* Hank Walker; *rt.* LIFE *photo by* Walter Sanders—Pictures Inc.
144, 145: LIFE *photos by* Walter Sanders *exc. t. rt.* LIFE *photo by* Hank Walker
147: LIFE *photo by* Walter Sanders
148, 149: B.S. *exc. bot. lt.*
150, 151: Acme, LIFE *photo by* John Phillips, Acme, Sovfoto—U. S. Army *photo* LIFE *photo by* N. R. Farbman, LIFE *photo by* Walter Sanders
152: W.W.
153: Keystone View Co.—Waldo Ruess
154, 155: LIFE *photos by* George Lacks *exc. bot. rt.* W.W.
156, 157: *t. rt.* LIFE *photo by* Carl Mydans—LIFE *photo by* James Burke, LIFE *photo by* Carl Mydans
158, 159: Sovfoto, Eastfoto
160, 161: LIFE *photo by* Carl Mydans, Acme—LIFE *photo by* Carl Mydans, LIFE *photo by* Johnny Florea
162: LIFE *photo by* David Douglas Duncan
163: Int., LIFE *photo by* Hank Walker
164: W.W.—Combine
165: Acme
166: W.W.
167: LIFE *photo by* Thomas D. McAvoy—W.W.
168, 169: Sovfoto (3)—Acme, LIFE *photo by* Margaret Bourke-White, Ewing Galloway
170, 171: *lt. col.* Acme—Marvin Koner *from* B.S. *for* Pageant Magazine—*rt.* W.W.; *rt. col.* Sovfoto, *map by* Rafael Palacios; *documents from* "Forced Labor In Soviet Russia" *by* David Dallin *pub. by* Yale University Press
172, 173: LIFE *photo by* William Vandivert, Sovfoto
174, 175: LIFE *photo by* Dmitri Kessel

Abbreviations: bot., bottom; cen., center; col., column; exc., except; lt., left; pub., published; rt., right; t., top. B.S. Black Star; Int., International; W.W., Wide World.